F]

BY

THE FEDS

To Cynthia,
May the Lord bless you
abundantly. I pray that
you are inspired by my
story. God Bless you

Truli Batiste

FLAGGED BY THE FEDS

A Spiritual Guide to Surviving Federal Prison

Trudi L. Batiste

For information contact:
www.trudibatiste.com

Publishing Consultant Irene Pro
Edited by Lori Hawkins
Book Cover Design by Irene Pro
Photo Credit: Unix Photography
Book Interior Design by Trudi Batiste.

Flagged by the Feds/ Trudi Batiste. -- 1st Ed.

Title ID:7399826
ISBN 978-1-9739-9981-2

Dedication

This book is dedicated to all of the ladies who I encountered along my journey. May God bless and keep you in His perfect peace until we meet again.

Continue to remember those in prison as if you were together with them in prison and those who are mistreated as if you yourselves were suffering.

HEBREWS 13:3 NIV

What People Are Saying...

Trudi Batiste is an amazing woman. Being in prison in Alabama was truly a horrible experience. Having Trudi as my bunkie made my life so much easier. We had respect for each other, and we have lots of love for our God above. She helped me reach out to Him, and because of her, I was able to build my relationship with our Heavenly Father. Without Him and without her guidance, I couldn't have made my life what it is today.

She was always there for me through my difficult times, and we became good Christian friends. She is my sister in Christ forever. Not only was she a wonderful friend while we were living in hell, Aliceville, she remained loyal when she left. That meant the world to me and my family. We are doing good. We have been struggling to get our lives back. We have come a long way, and we will make it someday. With God, all things are possible.

--Michele G. – Aliceville Prison Camp

Trudi is such an inspiration to me. It was a blessing to know a young woman who was not afraid to share her faith in God with others or to lend an ear and pray with someone. Working with Trudi in the salon was also a joy. I loved our conversations about Christ and the stories she shared about her life. What I remember most is how she continued to keep the faith and testified that she would get an early release. I witnessed how God came through for her. I was always blessed by her smile and by the way she let Jesus shine through.

--Cindy C. - Aliceville Prison Camp

To God be the glory for all the things He has done! God has a way of doing things! Never would've thought I would have been in that place, but God had a plan! I now realize that it was a "set-up." I had to be there to meet one of the most anointed, devil stomping, warring in prayer, and God-fearing woman!

When I met Trudi, I knew that God's hand was on her. It's not often that I immediately connect with someone, but when we began to talk about the goodness of Jesus, I realized this woman of God obtained *like precious faith*. At the time when we met, a divine connection was made. Some would look at us and think we were best friends like *Laverne and Shirley*, and others would see Elizabeth and Mary, as in the bible. God put us in a place where his Glory would be revealed...in prison.

Trudi is truly a sweetheart. She was one that I could turn my back on and not worry about a thing. We are friends for life. My sister, this is your season for God to use you for His Glory. The best is yet to come for you. Go forth in Jesus' name.

-- Helen S. – Aliceville Prison Camp

Adjusting to prison life was difficult for me. The people, the language, and the mentalities were foreign. Prison culture and the "outside" society are two different worlds. What worked in my professional life on the "outside" caused me to be ostracized, ridiculed, bullied and isolated inside prison. Trudi helped me to adjust to my new environment by looking for opportunities to grow spiritually, mentally and emotionally. She also directed my attention to focus on my true purpose for being here - God's assignment for my life. She blessed me beyond measure. –

--Michelle M.- Aliceville Prison Camp

The Holy spirit has put in the church many different spiritual gifts. He speaks to us through them. He gives God's messages to pastors, teachers, evangelists, and writers. He wants to use every Christian to tell about God. So amazing was my journey with Trudi Batiste when our paths crossed. On a journey like ours you ask God, why?

When I first arrived on the grounds of a Federal Bureau Prison Camp, I had a talk with God. I told God, 'I surrender all' to Him. I told Him, "I can't do this by myself!" To this day, I truly believe Trudi was my answer from God. It was like Jesus said in one of the parables about the shepherd who knows His flocks, I knew there was something special that set her far apart from the rest. It was something about the way she carried herself, the way she walked, the way she talked. It was the spirit of God in her. Trudi, gave me hope. If I needed a prayer she was there, a listening ear she offered. She was an anchor in my life to give me courage. Not only to me, but others here at the Aliceville Federal Bureau of Prison Camp.

Trudi's spiritual journey required a stop here at Aliceville where she made a difference. She became a greeter to the newcomers, whatever they needed she gave. If we needed hair care, again she was there. Spiritual guidance she also provided. As Trudi was readying her exit from this stop on her spiritual journey, she went around telling everyone, "I will stay in touch." In prison, you hear that a lot. With Trudi, it was different. E-mails arrived weekly with words of encouragement and scripture readings, not only for me, but also for others here at the camp. The words of encouragement and scripture were always on point for me; just what I needed for another day.

Trudi was, and is a blessing and spiritual gift in our lives. Thank you, my Christian friend, for the mark you left here at Aliceville Camp. Good luck with the launching of your new book. May God Bless and give you guidance. May this book be the beginning of many.

--L. Joye – Aliceville Prison Camp

There's really no way to explain how blessed I was to have met Trudi and to have her as a friend. From the very first day (October 31, 2014), she has been a positive influence in my life. She has been a friend who was there when I needed a shoulder to cry on and a protector of my secrets. She was a therapist when I needed emotional support and advice. She provided for me when it seemed no one cared, or they just didn't have the means to help me out. She was a personal hairdresser when I decided to let my hair grow because I couldn't manage it. But most of all, she has been a FIRST LADY, a true woman of God who always carried herself as she should and not once stepping out of character. I will always give her my utmost respect because she earned it. I can never thank her enough for being a true friend and spiritual advisor.

She never gave me the satisfaction of feeling sorry for myself or giving up. She always stepped in before I would go all the way down. She has been a blessing to so many. Our journey in Aliceville created special memories for me. I shed tears writing this as I remember the Friday nights in the salon that we shared singing, laughing, and talking. I remember she would dance like George Jefferson at the 10:00 pm count time; I couldn't stop laughing. Finding true friendship in such a terrible situation is one of the blessings that I thank God for. Trudi is definitely an advocate for all of the federal inmates of Aliceville, Alabama. I am so proud of her. She is a true friend and sister in Christ.

--Camille C.- Aliceville Prison Camp

TRU, my "Battle Buddy", GOD sent just for me! A true sister in Christ who is a Holy Spirit directed angel on this side of glory!

When I was up, I'd look for her, she delivered and comforted me with a Word from The Lord. When I was fair to middle, I'd look for her, she delivered and comforted me with a Word from The Lord. When I was down, I'd look for her, she delivered and comforted me with a Word from the Lord.

Trudi invoked in my soul, Proverbs 3:5, "to trust in The Lord, with all my heart, and to not lean on my own understanding" You see, when GOD has a work for you, He will send just who and what you need! When the student is ready, the teacher will come!

--Patricia H. – Aliceville Prison Camp

I came to prison in 2014 for identity theft and mail fraud. I didn't think I could make it to see my out date of 2018, but God stepped in. When I came to prison, I had nowhere to turn. I cried every day because I had left my 3 young boys at home, and I had just buried my father 3 days after I got sentenced. My mom had a stroke in June 2015; I couldn't be by her side. It seemed like my world had turned upside down. I was a total wreck, and then months later, my husband left me because he said I had nothing to offer him from prison. This was also very painful for me. I got on my knees and prayed to God to just give me strength to make it through. It didn't happen overnight but it happened.

I'm grateful and thankful for Trudi. She has been a very inspiring person to me. She always had to right words to say to me to uplift my spirit, and she helped me cope with a lot of stuff I was dealing with while incarcerated. She always stayed in touch with me once she left the prison grounds; she was always there. If I had anything that was on my mind, I could send her an email asking her to pray with me and for me. She always sends encouraging words and letters and cards. I can say that I am, and was truly BLESSED to have her in my circle while I was in bondage. God and Trudi made it happen for me. She showed me the light because I was in the darkness, and it seemed like I couldn't see my way through. I'm so thankful God placed her in my presence. He knew what I needed because of what I was going through. I pray that she continues to touch someone that is in darkness and in captivity.

Shantel M. – Aliceville Prison Camp

There are times in life when you cross paths with people, and you know it's divinely ordered. When Trudi first hit the campus, her spirit was so beautiful, but her physical beauty radiated even more! I officially met her at a prayer service for a friend who was being released. The anointing that was on her life to speak the things of God blew us all away and her voice to sing was even greater. A person of many talents is an understatement. She is an outstanding hairstylist, and yes, she became mine. We developed a sisterhood and would later sing in a gospel group together. Countless nights were spent sharing the things of God and talking about the plans God has for us. Was being where we were an *experience*? Definitely, but meeting a sister for life made it bearable! The fruit of her labor has now come to full fruition through the producing of this book. You are a true woman of God, and I am blessed to have you in my life. Run on Trudi and see what the end is going to be!

--Yolanda W. – Aliceville Prison Camp

I met Trudi at a low point in my life, a time when I was unsure of my future and what life held for me. Trudi was an inspiration to me because she treated me with kindness, and she showed me love and respect. She was always optimistic despite our surroundings. She told me that I should pray for contentment because I was going through a trial, and God would never bring me to something and leave me alone. I prayed for contentment, and I was at peace and had joy in my heart for the remainder of my time in Aliceville. I am home now and continue to pray for God's guidance and contentment until I get where He is sending me. Thank you Trudi!

--Verna A. – Aliceville Prison Camp

Acknowledgements

To my Lord and Savior, Jesus Christ: Thank you for entrusting me to fulfill the assignments given to me behind prison walls. I honor you in all that I do.

To my parents Frank and Janet Wynn and J. Donald Batiste: Thank each of you for being there for me every step of the way. From the bottom of my heart, thank you for everything. I love you forever!

To my Pastor and spiritual father, Bishop Melvin Williams, Jr: I am forever grateful for your unconditional love and support throughout much of my life's journey. Thank you for showing me what it means to truly forgive others.

To my sons, Troye, Alex, and Steven: Thank you for loving me through times when I wasn't the best role model. I am honored to be your mother and so proud to see your growth as men. Thank you for always believing in me. You are truly my greatest inspiration!

To my sister Carmen and my niece Camille: Thank you for being patient with me during my adjustment period after incarceration. I know it was A LOT…especially all of the crying spells. I appreciate you!

Many thanks to: Lucille, Traci, Val, Michelle, Nanora, Della, Lanny, Aaron, Andre, Jay, Dawn, Lucy, Lady Jacqui, Mesha, Camille, Claudia, Helen, Dorothy, Linda, Yolanda, Erica, Kitty, Cindy, Pat, and Thomas for your love, support, encouragement, and friendship during my darkest days. Words can never express my gratitude.

I am exceedingly grateful to God for two very special angels for their countless acts of love shown to me during my incarceration. Without them, serving time would have been extremely hard for me. Erika and Jerry, you were truly my lifeline. Thanks for holding me down in EVERY possible way without wavering. I will never forget your labor of love. May God return unto you a hundred-fold blessing!

Praise is continuously on my lips for all those who stand with me in prayer: To my extended family in Louisiana, my TOJ church family, and many devoted friends, thank you all for your support.

To my consultant Irene P. and editor Lori H. - Thank you for helping to make this book a reality. I salute you!

Contents

I magine waking up one day and finding yourself the subject of a federal investigation. Never could I conceive that prison would be part of my life's journey. For starters, I don't have the back story of those who society expects to end up incarcerated. For instance, I did not come from a broken home, nor did I struggle with addiction or live a life of crime. Sure, I had my share of teen drama growing up, but for the most part, life was good for me. So how on earth did I end up going to prison?

Prior to my incarceration, I didn't know how to value myself and lost my true identity, finding my worth only in trying to please others. I never learned that I had worth just as I was, so I was always seeking approval. I have come to believe that because of that, I allowed myself to be taken for granted, and said 'yes' when I should have said 'no.' The voids in my life led me to trust and seek approval from the wrong people. In the end, my denial and disobedience to God resulted in years of abuse, immeasurable suffering, and ultimately, a prison sentence.

Each of us has our own share of trials and challenges. When life presents circumstances beyond our control, we are left with vital choices to make. We can choose to hide and ignore our problems, or we can trust God, face them head on, and move forward. I have received God's forgiveness for my disobedience and allowed Him to restore me. A hard road to recovery remains, but it was in prison where I learned how to completely surrender, and to trust God in ALL things. I am both stronger and wiser for the experience, and all that I had to endure. I am a survivor!

In this edition, I share my story, expose my mistakes and reveal how I overcame trials that were meant to crush my spirit. In the process, I also summarize aspects of the federal prison system and provide valuable resources for you and your loved ones. As you begin this journey, it is my prayer that you overcome the fear and shame that may hold you hostage to poor judgements and past mistakes.

Know that we can find freedom in Jesus who delivers us from spiritual and physical bondage. You are not alone. *He whom the Son sets free is free indeed!* (John 8:36)

Chapter 1

RED FLAG!

THE NEWS THAT I WAS BEING charged with a crime was impossible for me to comprehend. It was like an out of body experience. I was in denial—and simply couldn't believe this was happening to me.

Should you ever find yourself facing criminal charges, my first piece of advice is this: humble yourself and rely on the wisdom of your Pastor or spiritual advisor, and the support of your family and close friends. Proverbs 11:14 says, *In the abundance of counselors, there is safety.* Do not make the mistake of trying to keep your dilemma a 'secret' from others. Make the details of your situation known to those who can assist you during this time. You may need their knowledge, resources, or finances. Recognize that you may not be thinking clearly, and you don't want to compound your problems by making poor decisions at this critical time. Give careful consideration to any offers of assistance or attempts to reach out to you, and do not be afraid to ask for help. Anticipate that some people will avoid you and even pass judgement against you. These reactions from others are normal and should be expected.

If you cannot afford a lawyer, know that a public defender can be just as knowledgeable on the points of law and the procedures at hand. Educate yourself on the federal criminal process so you can have substantial input and make informed decisions. Do not rely solely on the information provided by the lawyer when it comes to arriving at an outcome most favorable for you. Ask questions and be clear and realistic about what you are facing. This is not the time to 'check out' and depend on others to do the thinking for you. Your future is at stake!

There is a fallacy about public defenders not being good attorneys. I will just say this—good and bad exists in every line of work. In any field, some have a good work ethic, while others may take shortcuts. Some are skilled communicators who provide details, while others may summarize information based on their previous results. Still, there are those who fight on your behalf while appearing to fight against you.

This is true in federal service as well, and when the Federal authorities decide to pursue you, they will bring about whatever is needed to establish, strengthen, and prove their case—at times even if that means misrepresenting the truth. Your legal counsel becomes a mere a negotiator in the matter. It is critical that you establish a satisfactory rapport with the attorney representing you so you can achieve the most desirable results available.

When seeking to retain legal representation, a personal contact may recommend an attorney to you. Speaking personally, I suggest that you hire an attorney based on your own research. Most likely, your contact will make the recommendation to you based on their own personal experience or what they may have heard regarding another case. Keep in mind, what worked for someone else may not work for you. The specifics of your case and the outcome may well be completely different. There are specialties in any field, and the law certainly is no exception. Remember, whoever you choose to represent you will become your mouthpiece throughout the process. You must be able to trust your attorney to consider your input, be competent, and represent your interests at all times.

My first attorney was referred to me by someone who believed her to be one of the 'best' in her field. I accepted the recommendation without considering that the opinion was based on this person's personal experience with a specific instance. The outcome of that case was positive, but I learned later it was not even a federal court case. Because of our relationship and my inexperience, I failed to do my own due diligence and research the attorney's experience related to the type of case and jurisdiction involved. I would come to regret that decision, especially the fact that I ignored my gut instinct and made my decision based only on the credibility of another.

At my initial discussion with the lawyer, I felt what I would describe now as 'red flags,' but I overlooked them, feeling relieved to release my burden to one qualified to assist me. During this conversation, my lawyer reassured me that my case would be a priority for her. She insisted I contact her on her private cell phone number, and I was appreciative that she would accommodate my work schedule. She agreed to conduct our meetings via telephone as we were in different time zones. She forwarded the client contract which contained her fee information. Unfortunately, I was sold a dream. I would eventually find that out the hard way, soon after I paid my deposit.

During our next conversation, my attorney advised me she had spoken with the Assistant United States Attorney (AUSA). I was being charged with Conspiracy to Commit Mail Fraud.

Webster defines conspiracy as 'a secret plan made by two or more people to do something that is harmful or illegal.' The government maintained that the organization I was associated with had received monies but failed to use them for the purpose intended. Since I was listed as an Executive within the organization and my signature was on the Post Office Box that received the monies, I was named as a minor participant and co-conspirator in an alleged fraud.

I was devastated to learn what I was being accused of—particularly since I had volunteered my time to this group and received no salary for my work. In fact, I had invested my own finances in support of this organization, and certainly did not plot or plan anything illegal. Unfortunately, the feds opposed my contention and presented false scenarios to indicate otherwise.

I defended my claim to my attorney and she provided words of solace. She even shared with me some examples of her very own personal suffering, and her empathy confirmed my decision to hire her. I trusted that she was competent and would be my advocate. Unfortunately, this turned out to be careless on my part, and I ended up completely vulnerable, and naïve to the entire process. I wanted to trust her, and she seemed like the perfect person to defend me, but in the end, that was false and I paid the price.

It was a sudden and unexpected turn of events when my attorney's attitude abruptly changed towards me. The one person I trusted to defend me suddenly began to put limits on our communication. I was now required to work around her schedule. She proceeded to call my cell phone during my work hours. This meant that I would have to leave my desk and find somewhere to speak with her in private which was problematic. When I asked if she could call in the evenings so I could speak more freely, her response to me was, 'my schedule is 8 to 5,' which was inconsistent with her earlier promise of flexibility. Red Flag! I couldn't believe this was the same person that had been so accommodating before. Once again, I ignored my gut instincts and played by her rules. I also overlooked her use of profanity and her lack of professionalism during our conversations. I just wanted her to help me.

As time went on, the limited opportunity for communication with my attorney grew even more frustrating. The prosecuting attorney was playing dirty, trying to back me into a corner by threatening to arrest me at my place of employment. Meanwhile, I was planning to fight the charge and prove my innocence. I knew I had character witnesses and evidence to help with my defense.

I was allowed only ninety days from the date of the charge to decide whether to go to trial or accept a plea deal. But by now, my attorney seemed to only be interested in my payment, which was divided into three installments. She now didn't even acknowledge my text messages, emails or answer my calls until the week of a payment. When I contacted her office directly, the voicemail picked up. She mentioned an assistant though I was uncertain if one even existed. Any legal correspondence was sent to me via e-mail from an address that appeared to be her personal e-mail account. Her instructions to me were to write down my questions, but she would only address them the following month when her payment was expected.

I am sure by now you are wondering why I just didn't fire her. Well, let me explain this way, I had only a short time span to make very big life-altering decisions. Although the feds had worked over a year building a case against me, I had only this small window to prepare my argument. By the time her behavior had changed and my concerns had become serious, it was far too risky to chance starting over with someone else.

Let me stress again the importance of educating yourself, asking questions and listening to your own instincts. Don't let anyone who is supposed to be helping you, treat you badly. If your attorney becomes rude and impatient with you or otherwise makes you feel uncomfortable, speak up! This is YOUR LIFE and you deserve to be heard. If you cannot work out your concerns with your attorney—fire that one and quickly move on to someone who can get the job done. This is a decision that should be made only after careful consideration.

Retaining new counsel in the middle of any legal process is not ideal, especially when the stakes are so high. Your attorney should shape up, or you could threaten to inform the judge at your hearing. Look at the situation objectively to ensure your dissatisfaction is about the performance of the attorney—involving tangible things they can do or not do—rather than the potential outcome of your situation. For example, your attorney has a responsibility to both you and the court to provide you with information. Federal judges take the legal process very seriously and they want to make sure that you understand each step. If you agree to accept a plea, the judge will ask if your attorney has explained the agreement to you. Don't agree to sign anything that you don't fully understand. I made a bad choice when I continued to work with an attorney that I no longer trusted to work on my behalf. Don't make my mistake—trust your gut and rely on that *still, small voice* that speaks from within. (1 Kings 19:12).

Chapter 2

DESTINY INTERRUPTED

I WAS BORN IN LOUISIANA, in Baton Rouge, but moved to Virginia at the age of nine. I spent my summers back in Louisiana until I became a teenager. Once I was older, I didn't visit as often, only a few holidays here and there. At that point, the occasional wedding or other obligatory family visit was more than enough for me. Despite that, our family was considered close knit, and we regularly kept in touch by telephone.

However, for most of my life, being away from my family in Louisiana presented a void. Sure, I had connected with many friends growing up wherever I was, but they were not family. In the back of my mind, I always longed to be connected to my roots. My biological father, grandparents, aunts, uncles, and cousins—all of them were there. It was something about the southern hospitality that I wanted to experience more of. So, after thirty years of living in Virginia, I decided to move back to Louisiana.

When I made the move back to Louisiana, I hadn't disclosed details of what really prompted me to leave Virginia at that time.

I was too ashamed. Who would ever have believed that *I* was a victim of domestic abuse and was hiding from my abuser? Not me. I have been described as a smart, strong, self-sufficient woman, but never a victim. A single parent after the end of my first marriage, I worked ten times harder than ever before, to provide for myself and my three sons. I was driven, determined, and focused... then I met *him*.

We were together for seven years, and it seemed like each year our relationship got progressively worse. Early on, he was dishonest about many things regarding his situation, but of course, I didn't know that at the time. There were many smokescreens and variations of the truth, and by the time I fell in love with him, my heart was involved and I believed the lies he told me. I ended up investing everything I had in support of him. Over time, I became a victim of his physical, verbal, and emotional abuse. By the end of the relationship, I felt very used and my confidence was completely destroyed in the process. Once I relocated to Louisiana, I was finally free of him. Or, so I thought.

It was the fall of 2012, and I had been back in Louisiana almost a year, working full-time and pursuing my college degree. Things were looking up for me, and I was getting back to my happy self. One day I got home and found that a federal agent had left his card on my door with a message on the back urging me to contact him. Now, I will be the first person to say that no one wants a federal agent randomly showing up at their home. Honestly, due to increasing violence against men in our society I immediately became concerned, thinking there could be an issue with one of my sons. I silently prayed that the conversation would not be about either of them.

Heart racing, I reluctantly called the number on the card. *"What is this about?"* This is what kept running through my head, and what I asked the agent right away. My guard was up and I held my breath as I prepared myself to hear his answer. I was relieved when he told me it was about a previous employer of mine, and I felt myself begin breathing again. Though, he wouldn't give me any details over the telephone, the agent asked to meet me that evening, and I agreed to meet with him near my home. Inside, I heard the whisper of wisdom telling me to have a close companion accompany me.

When I arrived at the meeting place, the agent was parked in a black unmarked vehicle. I dialed his number again to announce my arrival. He exited his vehicle and we shook hands. After confirming my identity, he handed me a grand jury subpoena. Clearly perplexed, I opened the document. *"What is this? What does it mean?"* I quizzed. He still declined to provide me with any details, but instead gave me the contact number of a senior agent in Virginia.

The next day, I made the call to the senior agent. He was very cordial and thanked me for contacting him. I had never spoken to a federal agent before, and I will admit, I was a little nervous. I had never experienced legal issues in the past, or any previous interaction with law enforcement. I listened intently as he expressed interest in the ministry organization I had been affiliated with years before. He asked general questions regarding my role, and I explained to him that I had severed all ties with the members of the organization and the officers. Just hearing the name of the organization brought back painful memories—memories I was not inclined to immediately disclose to a stranger. Purposely, I neglected to tell him that the president of the organization was once my fiancé' and abuser.

Since I was living out of state, I arranged to meet with him the following month. He was extremely accommodating. He provided location details for the meeting and assured me that it would be nothing more than a casual conversation, and certainly not a grand jury hearing as the subpoena indicated. I don't know why I chose to believe him, but really, why wouldn't I? I also can't quite explain why my first response didn't include contacting an attorney. In my ignorance, I believed I could answer any questions regarding my role in the organization. I had nothing to hide, and honestly, it didn't occur to me to seek legal assistance.

The meeting was held at the Federal Building in downtown Richmond, Virginia, where a friend dropped me off at the corner. I entered through the metal double doors and headed towards the elevator. Exiting onto the specified floor, I was greeted by an armed security officer and receptionist. I had to pass through a metal detector which alarmed me at first, but then I thought, this is the federal building after all. The officer asked for my identification and requested my signature on the sign-in sheet. He said my ID would be returned when I signed out. The receptionist made a call and asked me to wait for a few moments. I was anxious, and really had no idea what I was walking into. Nonetheless, I tried to remain calm.

After a few minutes, a young, thin, blonde woman introduced herself as an Assistant US Attorney, and handed me her business card. She escorted me down a long hallway and we were met by the agent who I had been speaking with on the telephone. He also handed me his card which I slipped into my purse. They thanked me for agreeing to meet with them and we engaged in small talk as they led me to a conference area. Entering the room, I stood frozen as I faced five representatives from various government departments, all staring at me. At this point I was horrified, and I could feel my heart beating in my throat. This felt like an ambush and all I knew to do was pray, "Lord, help me!" I made a silent plea to my heavenly father before taking my seat at the head of the table, holding tightly to my purse. I'm sure they could sense my nervousness as they continued to glare at me. After the AUSA and FBI agent were settled in their seats, each person introduced themselves and passed me their business cards. The group included representatives from the Federal Bureau of Investigation, the Justice Department (AUSA), the Internal Revenue Service, the White-Collar Crime Division, and the United States Postal Service. I tried to maintain my composure as I waited for the introductions to end. A couple of the ladies smiled awkwardly at me, which only made me more uncomfortable. I was outnumbered to begin with, was the only person of color in the room, and felt extremely vulnerable and unprotected.

"Umm, do I need a lawyer?" I asked nervously, while trying to recall in my mind an episode of Law and Order.

"No, no, not at all. No need for concern. You did nothing wrong," was the answer of the AUSA. *"We just have a few simple questions for you."*

I felt my breathing slow down, but after walking into a situation that had been so badly misrepresented, I did not trust her.

***

The meeting began with the AUSA casually informing me of my legal rights. She said I was not required to answer anything I did not feel comfortable speaking about. Lastly, she reminded me that I could end the meeting at any time.

For nearly an hour, the AUSA asked questions about the mission of the organization and my specific role and duties. She questioned me about my ex-fiancé and his role. Although, we were apart, I passionately defended him and described the lives that had been positively affected because of his work in ministry. She presented me with some documents, many of which I recognized. I had created most of them in fact; things like membership forms, brochures, flyers and the like. A few I had never seen before, but she obviously didn't believe me. I reminded her that I had attended this meeting voluntarily and had no reason to lie. At that point, she began to raise her voice and use profanity, but I didn't react and continued to deny her accusations. The room was quiet and they all still glared at me. It was her next statement that drove me into complete shock. She stated that my ex had contacted her office and made accusations about me. I felt my heartbeat racing again and I was done defending myself. I requested a restroom break—I had to get out of there! I could feel the tears building up and I wanted to call my mother.

My plans to make the call were thwarted when two of the women accompanied me to the restroom. I tried to delay, taking my time hoping they would leave me there alone. It became obvious they were waiting for me and I struggled to think of a way to end the meeting. I texted my friend from inside and asked her to pick me up. I stressed that if I was not outside within 20 minutes, she should alert my parents.

I exited the stall and the two ladies were casually leaning against the wall, chatting. I washed my hands and they led me out of the restroom—one in front and the other followed behind me. I was still processing the AUSA's last statement to me, and replayed in my head the words my ex had spoken to me in anger some three years prior.

"I hate you! I am going to destroy you if it is the last thing I do!"

He was angry with me because I had ended the relationship, and he accused me of trying to sabotage his organization. Regardless of how much help I was to him, I could not pretend anymore. I had allowed him to manipulate me for the last time. In the past, when I threatened to leave him, he continued to exercise his complete control over me and eventually found his way back into my heart. Studies show there are three cycles of abuse—the first, a tension building phase, is where the verbal abuse begins. During the second phase, the tension peaks and physical violence may result. Finally, the honeymoon phase is when the abuser becomes ashamed and remorseful for their behavior. It is during the final phase that the abuser convinces the victim the abuse will not continue, and the victim reluctantly remains in the toxic relationship. I had been through this cycle many times before finally deciding to leave, even if it meant risking my life.

I returned to the conference room and asked for a drink of water. I tried to remain calm, but I was ready to end the 'casual conversation' that had suddenly turned into an interrogation. Before the AUSA could decide to resume her questions, I blurted out, *"This meeting is over!"*

I noticed everyone taking short glances at one another, so I gathered my belongings and stood up. The conversation would have to continue without me. When the AUSA and Federal Agent stood up, I darted towards the door. They thanked me again for my time and I rushed down the hall to retrieve my ID. As I exited the building, my friend was waiting for me in the car. I burst into tears, wishing I had sought advice and gotten a lawyer to represent me.

***

Several months passed after that day and I had heard nothing more from the Feds. I resumed my regular activities of work and school. The meeting had left me stressed, and I was so thankful when things returned to normal for me. Gradually, my concern receded and at this point, I didn't expect to ever hear from them again.

Meanwhile, life in Louisiana was not the fairy tale I had imagined it to be when I was living in Virginia longing to move back. I come from a large family, and had been excited at the prospect of re-connecting with my cousins. As kids, we were all very close, but life had changed. For one thing, we were adults with our own families now. I had hoped we would be close again—especially now that I was living there. I needed their support more than ever. But since I had chosen to keep certain things private, they had no idea I had endured years of abuse or the fact that I was currently struggling financially trying to make it on my own. The worst part was acting like I was okay, even though I was living in the 'hood.' I had never had to live in such a place before, but I had no choice because it was all I could afford at the time.

The first Monday of 2014, nearly two years later, I received an email from the federal agent in Virginia. I remember that very specifically because on New Year's Eve, I had posted something on Facebook about being happier than I had ever been before. I had gotten a new promotion at work and my 'hood' apartment had been turned into a place I could be proud to come home to. I put off calling the agent for two days before I finally got up the nerve to do it. I nearly fainted when he told me the purpose of his call. He said that the Commonwealth of Virginia was going to charge *me* with a crime.

"I, I don't understand. I did nothing wrong," I pleaded with him. Before ending the call, he apologized to me.

"Ma'am, a word of advice, find yourself a lawyer… a good one." The next thing I remember was falling on the floor.

Chapter 3

DO YOUR RESEARCH

I CAN'T EMPHASIZE THIS ENOUGH—DON'T just rely on your attorney's education. You should do your own study on the federal law process, (or whatever jurisdiction you find yourself in). Ask questions. Don't give your approval of anything you don't accept or understand. Your attorney bears a responsibility to discuss all your concerns before you go to court, and you have a right to question actions that you don't agree with. Ask *the Holy Spirit to guide you into all truth* regarding your situation (John 16:13). The bible states that *people perish for lack of knowledge* (Hosea 4:6), and *in all thy getting, get an understanding* (Proverbs 4:7). Apply the knowledge and try to gain full understanding regarding the details of your case.

Read and clearly comprehend all documents before signing them. Here are a few more useful tips:

- Research the attorney's experience and their success rate with 'federal' cases. You will need a criminal attorney—

not civil. Ask if he or she has ever argued a case involving the crime you have been charged with. Google them. Check for reviews and comments. Determine if there have been any grievances or sanctions against them with the bar association.

- Arrange to meet with the attorney in person before electing to hire him or her. Bring someone along whose judgement you can trust. Though an attorney may prefer a telephone consultation to review specifics of your case, know that a good one will always want to set up a face-to-face meeting.

- Establish a good rapport with the attorney, but also seek a peaceful spirit about hiring them. Ultimately, whoever you choose should make every effort to reach the best outcome possible. You need absolute certainty that your best interest is the paramount concern of your legal team when the time comes.

- Make certain that your attorney does not operate completely alone. Lawyers who do not have a team of paralegals to support them, may not be able to address the workload of your case. Your file may just become one of many shuffled from day to day.

- Require updates in a 'timely' manner. This level of expert assistance will cost you more, but it is something you deserve in order to feel confident in your counsel and to put your mind at rest. This is your *life* and you can never set a value on your freedom.

- Read all that you can about what to do when you have been charged with a crime. Become familiar with the legal terminology and with the Federal Guideline Chart. If found guilty, the extent of your sentence will essentially be based on this chart. (we will deal with this in a later chapter).

- Communicate with others who have had federal court cases. They can possibly address other questions you may have. The more knowledge you have, the more familiar you will be with your attorney's process. Follow up with research to verify what you can.

- Ask your attorney about his or her relationship with Federal Court Judges. If the experiences are positive, this may work in your favor. Like the old quote says, "It's not what you know, but who you know." Lawyers can have impact—positive or negative—based on their credibility, integrity, and acquaintance with the court.

- Find out your attorney's means of communication and the frequency in which they provide updates. What is the expected turnaround time in responding to requests? Your lawyer must meet important deadlines when filing time sensitive papers in federal court. Failure to do so can hinder your case.

- Don't be afraid to assert yourself to your attorney if you are not pleased with his or her performance. Retain new counsel if unavoidable. Follow your instincts and address all red flags immediately!

Chapter 4

GOING THROUGH MOTIONS

IN THIS CHAPTER, I WILL present an overview of the Federal Criminal process. The intent is to provide a broad understanding only. Please know that your case may not involve all the steps that I have outlined.

Once an offense is brought to the attention of federal authorities (Feds), an investigation gets underway. The Feds only become involved when the crime violates federal law. Subpoenas may be requested from the grand jury to facilitate collection of reports from suspects and/or witnesses as a part of the investigation.

THE GRAND JURY

Most federal criminal charges must be presented before the grand jury. Consisting of individuals from the community, the grand jury reviews and examines evidence submitted to them by the U.S. Attorney's Office, which is part of the Department of Justice. The grand jury hearing is held in strict confidence and no one is present except for the members of the jury, the court reporter, and a witness. When evidence has been heard, the grand jury will determine whether a crime has been committed. In *most* instances, a grand jury will determine that there is probable cause (reasonable grounds) of a wrong having been carried out. Once this has been established, written charges—known as an indictment—are issued. Co-defendants may be named in one indictment. If the indictment alleges multiple offenses, each separate crime is specified as a 'count.' Co-defendants may also be charged on specific counts.

State court operates differently. In state court, the client and the attorney will be present at the probable cause hearing. Unlike federal court, your attorney will have an opportunity to interview any witnesses.

INITIAL APPEARANCE

When an indictment is filed with the court, the party or parties named must voluntarily appear—or be arrested. The initial appearance before a judge is usually within 72 hours of the arrest. If you voluntarily surrender, you must be present before the court and move through the booking process as if you were arrested. This includes being fingerprinted and photographed. The magistrate judge will then advise you of the charge(s), the maximum penalty that each charge carries, and your rights. You will have the right to remain silent and the right to have an attorney to represent you. If you cannot afford to retain your own attorney, the court will determine if you qualify to have a court appointed lawyer.

The magistrate judge will also determine if you are to be held with or without a bail bond. After a person is arrested, the court sets a release amount based on the offense. For example: if the bail amount is $1000, a bail bondsman will arrange with the court for your release in exchange for a bond. Some courts will accept 10% or in this example, $100. This is a way of ensuring that you appear for court once you have been released from police custody. The bail bondsmen will be responsible for you and make sure you appear on your court date.

If you are held without bond, a detention hearing will be scheduled and the magistrate has four options regarding your release:

- **You may be released on your own recognizance**—this means that you must promise before the judge to attend your future court hearings.
- **Released with restrictions**—this may involve electronic monitoring (house arrest), curfew, drug testing, or require that you hold consistent employment.
- **Temporary detainment** until bail is posted.
- **Detainment while you await trial**—the judge may decide against releasing you for the following reasons: prior criminal history, failure to appear in the past, probation violation, you pose as a threat, or you are believed to be a flight risk.

ARRAIGNMENT

At this hearing, you will appear with your lawyer and be advised of your rights, the charges that you face, and the penalty for each charge. You will receive a copy of the charge, and you may enter a plea in response to the charges. If your attorney has not negotiated a plea agreement, your lawyer will probably plead 'not guilty' on your behalf until he or she can review the case with you.

MOTIONS AND DISCOVERY

Papers filed by both your defense attorney and the prosecution that ask the court to do something within your case are called 'motions.' For example, a motion may be filed requesting to 'continue' your case to a later date. The judge can either approve or deny the motion request.

Before proceeding to trial, you can request material or 'discovery' about your case from the prosecutor. This information will include any evidence that they claim to have against you. Keep in mind—by law—the government does not have to provide you with evidence until you decide to proceed to trial. Work closely with your attorney to help with your defense.

Be completely honest and provide your counsel with names of all who can assist in proving your case. If the government has charged you, they most likely have everything that they need to take you to trial. They have had years to complete their investigation. Your attorney may have had only 30 to 60 days to review details of your case and discuss options with you prior to moving forward. The process may not seem fair. Unfortunately, this is how the system works.

PLEA BARGAIN

This is one of the most serious and challenging decisions that you will have to make, and you—and only you—can make it. What you decide will permanently affect your future, so take your time and review the specifics thoroughly. You should determine what is most valuable to you—your freedom or your reputation? Consider this, your reputation was marred the instant you were charged with the crime. If your face flashed across the television screen or if someone saw the newspaper article, you were the hot topic among family and friends at the very least, and likely a wider circle than that. I valued my freedom more than my reputation, and concluded that the Feds would stop at nothing short of imprisoning me one way or another, robbing me of years with my loved ones. By the way, they play dirty. Many times, a conviction can lead to a promotion within the office of the Prosecutor.

Per the United States Sentencing Commission, in 2014, 97.1% of all convicted offenders pled guilty. In my opinion, plea agreements are the reason that the FBI success rate is so high, not because the matter was decided in court. When the prosecuting attorney threatened to have me arrested and to attach additional charges when I opted to go to trial, I determined that my freedom was more important to me. I pled guilty to avoid additional prison time. I was comforted by those who love me and know my true character, and I chose to worry less about the opinions of others.

Your attorney may be able to negotiate certain items in the plea agreement, although most are standard. For instance, I asked for some of the language to be replaced in my final draft. I was denied because my lawyer missed the deadline to file. When the court approves your signed agreement, you will be given a sentencing date. If your plea agreement is rejected, you will proceed to trial. Remember, in the end, the decision is always at the discretion of the judge.

GOING TO TRIAL

At the trial, the government and the defense present evidence that will either prove or disprove the charges against you. The government must be able to prove their case beyond a reasonable doubt. During the trial, a victim or witness may be called to testify that harm was done to them because of a crime.

Jurors will be selected to listen to the evidence and decide your case. The jury is made up of twelve members of the community. The jury will be given specific instructions when reviewing the details of your case. You are presumed innocent until proven guilty. After the evidence has been heard, the jury will reach a verdict.

SENTENCING

Should you be found guilty of any of the counts included in the indictment the judge can detain you immediately, but most will choose to impose sentence at a later date. While you are waiting to be sentenced, a pre-trial services officer will be assigned to you and he or she will conduct a complete background investigation. The officer may also perform an interview with you about your entire life history. You should request that your attorney be present for this interview, if possible. This information will be used to create a report called a pre-sentencing report (PSR) or a pre-sentencing investigation (PSI) report.

The report can be approximately 30 to 100 pages long and will be submitted to the judge. It will provide a snapshot of who you are to the court, because you won't have an opportunity to introduce yourself. This report will also follow you to prison and will be the "most important document" in your file. It is essentially your life on paper and describes your character to the court and prison officials based on the testimonies of others. You will be profiled based on the information that is provided. Included are details of your life spanning from your first childhood memory to your most current status. The sections of the report include more personal details, such as date of birth, education, employment history, medical condition, psychological status and a complete financial history. Any information you provide to the officer will be verified. You will also have to disclose personal information about your immediate family members. Your parents and even former spouse will be contacted to verify the information and to discuss your character and personal relationships.

Having to recall such intimate details of your life is a very uncomfortable process. You will also be required to discuss the crime that you have been found guilty of, and reveal whether you accept responsibility. It takes approximately thirty days for the officer to complete the report. Once this report has been completed, you and your lawyer should meet to go over the report with a fine-tooth comb to check for errors or discrepancies. You will want to paint the most positive and accurate picture of yourself when describing your background.

The end of the report will list details of the crime and the results of the government's investigation against you. Ironically, my report states that there was no evidence that I had participated in any wrongdoing or that I was even aware of it. I was simply guilty by association... thus the term 'conspiracy,' which means you can be charged for something someone else did. See what I mean about playing dirty? Based on the results of the investigation, the pre-sentencing officer will make a recommendation for sentencing as shown on the United States Sentencing Guidelines Chart.

Your PSR will show a number called your 'base offense level' and also show how this number was calculated. Once you know that number, you can refer to the guidelines chart and find the range of months of imprisonment for your offense. The judge can sentence you on the low end, the high end or anywhere between. After reviewing your PSR, the judge may conclude that because you are an educated individual with great professional experience, you should have known better. Thus, you could receive maximum penalties. Or, conversely, that it was a single lapse in judgement amidst an otherwise upstanding life, and lean toward the minimum sentence. It's all at the judge's discretion.

Be sure to disclose in your interview any information that may have caused a lapse in judgement, such as a mental disorder, stress, physical or mental abuse, or substance abuse. Do not be embarrassed to document this. This is not the time to let pride get in the way. If you have a history of drug abuse, you may also qualify for early release treatment programs. The judge may recommend a program if the abuse is documented in your report.

During the investigation, the pre-trial officer will speak with any victims of the alleged crime. The victim may provide a written account, called a victim impact statement, describing how he or she was affected by the crime. The statement will be reviewed by the judge and become a permanent part of your criminal record. The pre-trial services officer will also take a tour of your home to confirm that you in fact live in the home, and will want to see where you keep your belongings. He or she will check to make sure there are no weapons or drugs in the home. While on pre-trial release, you must continue employment and your behavior will be monitored. It is best to sever any ties that you have with other convicted felons, especially if you suspect they may be involved in criminal activities. Obey all instructions. Seriously, don't play with these guys or give them anything to use against you. All the cards are in their hands.

As a part of your sentence, your punishment may include probation, community service, or imprisonment. Unfortunately, my lawyer had me thinking I was eligible for probation, but I later found out that based on the sentencing guideline chart and my base level score, probation was never even an option for me.

If you are sent to prison, you may be allowed to return to the community—under supervision—after your release, perhaps even before you've completed all the time sentenced. You will be required to report to your probation officer within 72 hours. You may also have to spend time in a halfway house as a part of your release. Either way, you must abide by the rules. You may also be given additional restrictions such as a curfew or a requirement to obtain permission before leaving the state. In some cases, regular drug testing will also be required. If you don't follow the terms of your probation, you could end up back in prison for the duration of your sentence. In addition, breaking the rules of your probation could result in new charges, adding time to your sentence.

Lastly, the court may also impose a fine or order the defendant to pay restitution to help alleviate financial losses for the victim if applicable.

Chapter 5

LAW AND ORDER

YOU CAN NEVER PREDICT WHAT will happen when you get to court. In my experience, it is better to be prepared for the worst. My base level number was 19, and although the charge carried a sentence of 60 months (5 years), my recommended sentence range on the sentencing chart was between 30-37 months. According to the guidelines, I was in a zone D felony class and therefore not eligible for probation or home detention. My criminal history was category 1, meaning that I had none. The prosecutor added a statement to my pre-sentencing report (PSR), saying that although my likelihood of committing a crime in the future was very low, I should be punished just like anyone else charged with this crime. It was determined and documented that my role was "minor."

Unfortunately, your good deeds, character, integrity or other traits will not be included in the report. It is all black and white, and this summary of your entire life is what a judge will base his or her decision on. That, as well as the stated opinions of those who don't even know you, such as the prosecuting attorney and federal investigators. Keep this in mind during your pre-trial interview. When you review your report, you want to alert your attorney to any errors or discrepancies. If corrections need to be made, your attorney must contact the pre-trial investigator so that the prosecutor is notified of the change. If the government won't agree to change the report, the judge will decide. By the time you are sentenced, you will be so emotionally drained from the entire process that you'll just want the whole thing to be over and done.

I was classified as a first-time, non-violent offender with no prior criminal history, so in my ignorance, I expected the judge would suspend any recommended prison time. Worst case scenario, I would be on probation and be required to pay a ridiculously large fine. As you can imagine, I was completely blindsided and devastated when the judge sentenced me to thirty months in federal prison. Yes, two years and six months is what the government recommended for me.

Once I got over the initial shock that I was now a 'convicted felon,' and would actually be incarcerated, I had only thirty days to handle my personal affairs before having to surrender to a federal prison camp. Based on my personal experience, I discovered that many attorneys are not familiar with the Bureau of Prisons procedures once sentencing is complete. I was able to find only limited information online to prepare me for what I had to face. I found many books written by men, but the female prison perspective is much different. I searched for a book that would provide me with valuable information and describe what I should expect.

I used my time in prison to document my experiences since I wasn't able to find anything currently published that wasn't another version of *Orange is the New Black*. Based on my research and experience, here are some tips that would have been helpful to me in preparation:

- **Surround yourself with positive people who will encourage you and not join in a pity party.** This is a very emotional time and you should be around those who will labor in prayer both with and for you. Rely on those who will exert strength when you have moments of weakness. For me, those people were my Pastor, my parents, my children, and a select group of loyal friends. My Pastor covered me in prayer and my friends surrounded me with positive energy, even though we were all hurting. My parents and children provided me with the love and care I needed to get me through the next phase of my process. I couldn't move forward with a clear mind until all those pieces were in place.

- **Prepare yourself mentally for departure.** If the United States Attorney recommends incarceration, it is *highly likely* that some prison time will result. It's just a matter of determining *when* you will have to go. Your time is precious so don't waste it. Get busy getting your affairs in order.

- **Tell your family and friends**. If you have children and have not discussed your fate with them, take the opportunity to arrange a family meeting with your loved ones. Be honest, so everyone can be made aware and can prepare for the next steps. If you have younger school-aged children, consult with loved ones to determine the best approach and make sure everyone is saying the same thing. You don't want to alarm your children or say anything that might cause undue trauma, so use careful wisdom.

- **Arrange for a caregiver who is willing and able to take on the role of parenting your child in your absence.** This person should be responsible and open to maintaining lines of communication between you and your children. Initially, I discussed everything with my older children as things progressed. I delayed telling my youngest son until I was certain that there was a chance I would go to prison. I devoted myself to spending quality time alone with him to discuss the situation in private. My ex-husband and I arranged a time with him to share the most important facts. We were honest with our son about the possible outcome—that prison could be a definite possibility. Let me pause here for a moment. To be prepared is exercising wisdom, not acceptance. Know that whatever your outcome, it is God who is in control. It is wise to have a conversation with your children and not avoid it by choosing to be in denial.

- **Don't be defeated by guilt.** Although unfortunate, this situation is very real and you can't waste time being depressed and scared. This is the time to armor yourself in the Lord (Ephesians 6:11) and prepare for the journey ahead. The enemy will come to bring fear and discouragement, but you must fight against his lies. Expose the enemy by being honest about your situation and don't be held hostage by thoughts of what others think of you.

- **Try not to be ashamed or embarrassed by what you are facing**. Accept help from those willing to offer you their support, information, and even finances. If you made a mistake, admit it and ask the Lord for forgiveness and move on. If you have been falsely accused, make your own decisions regarding your freedom and be free from the opinions of others! Either way, don't let the enemy silence you by keeping your ordeal a secret.

- **Connect to men and women of faith and attend a church regularly.** If you have not already done so, re-commit your life to the Lord and begin to lay the foundation that will sustain you in the days to come. Read the bible scriptures daily, even if it's just one verse. A good place to start is in the Book of Psalms. Find a verse in the bible for your situation and memorize it. Proverbs 3:6 says, *In all your ways acknowledge Him, and He will direct your path.* You will get through this; your relationship with God promises, *He will never leave you nor forsake you.* (Hebrews 13:5)

When you get to prison, you will need all the support and encouragement you can get. There are places of worship and special services in prison where you can come together with others of similar faith. Prison is not filled with just criminals and con artists. There are many there who, just like you, love God and are serving Him… even behind prison walls.

I surrounded myself by positive, praying friends and family. I attended regular weekly church services and bible study, right up until the day I reported to prison. Each passing day, I gained the strength and courage that equipped me for my journey. *Faith comes by hearing the Word of God* (Romans 10:17). Connect to people of faith and don't allow negative conversations to infect your spirit.

- **Appoint someone over your financial matters**. Sit down with this person to discuss your financial situation. Discuss payment plans for your recurring monthly expenses, such as mortgage, car payment, car insurance, etc. Consider directing this person to put aside funds on behalf of your children in the case of emergency. If you are a single person and renting your home or apartment, notify your landlord and request to rent from month to month. What explanation can you provide without disclosing details? You can tell them simply that a personal family matter has occurred which may require you to move soon.

If your recommended sentence is for a longer period, you may want to consider renting or selling your home. You should legally appoint someone responsible to handle your business affairs. Explain your wishes and how you want them to proceed on your behalf in each situation. If you are married, you, along with your spouse, should prepare a written plan for each month that you are away. Work together and discuss ways to maintain your current financial status and/or discuss your options. If possible, you should put aside funds to assist with your prison stay. Show appreciation for any monies your supporters can contribute to you. Trust me—you WILL need them at some point, so inform them of your needs ahead of time and pray that they come through for you.

MAKE A TO-DO LIST

If you are going away for more than a year, you should consider doing whichever apply from the following list. Once your affairs are in order, you can devote your time to moving forward with a clear head.

- Cancel subscriptions such as magazines, Netflix, Amazon, Hulu, etc.
- Cancel automatic bill payments and auto renewals.
- Arrange for cell phone service to be cancelled as soon as 24 hours after you surrender to prison.
- Withdraw your cash and close your active checking accounts.
- Pay off credit cards. You will not be able to apply for new credit until you are off probation. Supervised release can range from 3-10 years.
- Pay off outstanding debts as possible.
- Collect addresses, telephone numbers and email addresses of persons you wish to contact while you are away.
- Purge your wardrobe, pack your belongings, and label them to be stored away with someone you can trust.
- Don't create any new debt. Your credit report will be monitored.
- Cancel any recurring appointments and memberships (such as gym, hairstylist, dentist, primary care physician, etc.)
- Arrange a date to end your employment in good standing if possible. You are encouraged to work until your departure, but there is a chance that your employer may

terminate you once they find out you have been charged with a crime.

- If you own a vehicle, consider selling it and use the funds toward care of your children or other high priority expenses.
- Give away or sell household furnishings.
- Forward your mail to someone who is trustworthy.
- If needed, ask your attorney or pre-trial services officer to recommend psychological counseling services for you during this time.
- Schedule a visit for a routine doctor and dentist appointment prior to departure.

Chapter 6

COUNTDOWN TO SENTENCING

TIME WILL MOVE QUICKLY AS you grow nearer to your sentencing day. *Trust in God and lean not to your own understanding* no matter what you are facing (Proverbs 3:5-6). The prosecutor's goal is to convict you; they will not be concerned about your physical, mental, or emotional state.

There were moments throughout these days when I had crying spells. I scheduled an appointment with a counselor and was prescribed treatment to help me rest. There were days when I was overwhelmed by anxiety and was given medication. The subconscious mind is very powerful and I highly suggest counseling if needed. The humanistic part of you may try to override your confidence in God. You may even be challenged in your emotions by discouragement and signs of depression; know that this is a natural part of the process. Please seek professional help immediately if you experience suicidal thoughts.

The government may ask you to provide information that would assist them in continuing their investigation against others associated with your case. If you are cooperative, the prosecuting attorney can propose to the judge a 5K Rule or downward departure. These approved motions would provide the judge a way to sentence you below the recommended sentencing range if he or she so desires, which would reduce the time of your confinement.

In exchange for your assistance, the prosecutor may file a 'Rule 35 Motion' on your behalf, if your assistance to the government is deemed 'substantial.' Keep in mind, this reduction in your sentence is at the government's discretion, including the determination of what is considered 'substantial.' To some, it may be advantageous to receive this sort of reduction, but be certain that you fully understand and accept the process and that your lawyer is experienced and can negotiate on your behalf. Remember, the prosecution is not concerned about saving you, and they will fabricate details to get information from you. Use your own sound judgment and confer with your attorney before sharing any information about others. Take responsibility for your own role in the events that led to the charges and conviction. By doing so, you are eligible to obtain a 2-point reduction of your base offense level number, which may cut down your confinement.

Discuss the matter of character witnesses with your lawyer. Having credible character witnesses speak on your behalf or character statements read at your sentencing could influence the judge in your favor. Since the judge does not know you personally, your witnesses can portray you in a positive light and describe your bonds with others. Your lawyer should meet with your witnesses prior to court and prepare them to speak at your sentencing.

Look up all available prisons within 500 to 700 miles from your home. Your attorney can ask the judge to designate you to the facility nearest your family—though this is not a guarantee. If no probationary issues remain at the time of your sentencing—such as outstanding warrants or arrests—you may be given permission to self-surrender to prison in 30 days or more. The judge will inform you at the sentencing hearing.

If you have a history of substance abuse (alcohol, illegal drugs, or prescription drugs) you may be eligible for the Residential Drug Abuse Program or RDAP. The RDAP program, when successfully completed, can take up to 12 months off your prison sentence. Details of your abuse must be recorded in your PSR for you to qualify. High security (violent) inmates are excluded from the RDAP. The judge will make a recommendation if you are eligible, but always discuss your options with your attorney.

After you have been sentenced, you will be sent a letter detailing where and when you must report to prison. If you are unable to arrange for someone to transport you, you must report to the U. S. Marshals and be held in the local jail to await transport. I firmly advise you to arrange your own transportation to the prison and NOT surrender to the U.S. Marshals. If you are remanded at sentencing, you will have no alternative except to wait in a local jail until you are taken to your designated facility which can take weeks or even months.

You will be required to pay a court assessment fee. If you are unable to make the payment prior to going to prison, it will be subtracted from your prison salary. More on this later.

While waiting for your official designation package, continue to prepare yourself by doing the following:

Research the website of the prison closest to you. Familiarize yourself with the policies in the online orientation booklet. Know as much as you possibly can about your facility before you arrive. Many procedures are the same for each prison, but you need to be familiar with the rules at your actual designation facility.

Finalize your list of contact information for friends, acquaintances, and family members. This should include addresses, emails, and telephone numbers. Make copies of the list, take one with you to prison and leave a copy with a friend to mail to you if needed.

Finalize your cell phone cancellation to end 24 hours after you surrender, once you have a definite date. Use your phone to say your final goodbyes as you are travelling to your destination.

Begin a magazine subscription 1 week prior to your self-surrender date. Most subscriptions start within 4 weeks. I recommend www.inmatemagazineservice.com

Create a list of books you want friends and loved ones to send to you over time. Check the rules of your prison because some will only accept books that are shipped in brand new condition directly from the publisher.

If you have not received your designation package in the mail, begin checking the Bureau of Prisons website each day (www.BOP.gov) to see if your name has been entered into the federal system. Enter your first and last name in the 'inmate locator' field. If you are shown in the system, the message 'not in BOP custody' may appear under your name. You will be able to identify your inmate register number which will be your identification number when you arrive to prison. MEMORIZE IT. This number is required for EVERYTHING you do in prison. You'll need to know it when you first arrive.

Wean yourself off habit-forming items. For example, coffee, nicotine, caffeine, over the counter medication, prescription sleep aids, sugar, chocolate, and any other indulgences. Your transition will be much easier if you aren't having to do this all at once after you arrive.

Change your diet to basic nutritious items, and begin eating in a healthier way. Prison's use the BOP national menu which you can find online.

Exercise. Schedule at least 30 minutes a day to do cardio and walking. Also, do strength exercises and crunches. Some facilities require a lot of walking to get from one building to another, so try to get in shape before you go.

STAY POSITIVE! Don't let stress get the best of you. Stay prayerful. Continue to talk to God about your fears and receive His comfort. Seek Him daily in the Word and stay connected to Him. Surround yourself with your support system. Do not isolate yourself. Partner with someone who will pray with you each day. Remain quiet before the Lord and devote yourself to fasting and prayer so that you are in tune and alert for the journey ahead. Remember: *NO FEAR, ALL FAITH* (2 Corinthians 5:7; Isaiah 43:1-2).

One day BEFORE you report to prison.

- Look on your prison's website for instructions on how to send inmate mail to your facility. Mail yourself a copy of your contact list and pictures. Most facilities allow up to 25 photos. DO NOT send any of your legal documents. Address the envelope exactly as indicated on the website. Don't forget to include your Register ID Number. You will need to know your register number to receive your incoming mail and packages.

- Mail a money order to yourself at the BOP lockbox account. You will need money in your account when you arrive to prison. Sometimes there is a delay in processing funds which can keep you from getting the things that you need. I suggest having a minimum of $50 in your account and no more than $500 per month. Money sent to the lockbox usually posts to your account within 3 days. The National Lockbox address is: Federal Bureau of Prisons, Post Office Box 474701, Des Moines, Iowa 50947-0001. Include your name and register number on the envelope and a United States Post Office money order.

- Keep in mind, monies coming into your BOP account will be monitored. If you have been ordered to pay restitution, you will be required to pay minimum of $25 every three months. If large amounts consistently post to your BOP account, you may be required to make larger payments toward your restitution monthly. Try to control how much money is sent to you. Make sure to keep just enough in your account to handle your monthly expenses.

Federal prison is very costly. Many have a misconception that three meals and a bed is sufficient. However, if you are fortunate enough to be able to take advantage of all the 'extras' that prison offers, it will cost you. Monthly expenses include commissary items, with a spending allowance up to $320. E-mail is available at 5 cents a minute for both incoming and outgoing, up to $30, and phone calls are approximately $3.15 for 15 minutes. You are allowed only 300 phone minutes per month, regardless of how much money is in your account. You may receive an extra 100 minutes during the Thanksgiving and Christmas months.

There are inmates who do not receive any financial assistance from family, so they offer services to support themselves. These services are not authorized by the prison; however, some services include: hairstyling, nail art, ironing uniforms, housekeeping, etc. The basic essentials such as soap, deodorant, toothpaste, combs, sanitary items and razors are provided to indigent inmates once a month. Items may vary at each prison.

- Purchase a $25 money order to take to the prison with you. If you are not allowed to bring the money order, as a safeguard, have a family member send you money at a Western Union or Money Gram immediately after they leave you. Wired money will post to your account within 15 minutes. The information on how to complete the form is on the BOP website under 'send inmate money.'

Trust me, you need to utilize all of the above options so you have money in your BOP account when you get inside. You don't want to depend on anyone for anything in prison. In most cases, you will need to have funds posted to your account to make the first phone call to your family. You also need funds available to purchase personal items if allowed to shop at the commissary when you first arrive.

Chapter 7

SURRENDERING ALL

I RECEIVED MY DESIGNATION PAPERS about five days before my actual surrender date. I was hoping I would only have to drive five hours away to the Alderson, West Virginia prison camp. I had studied the facility and shared the website information with my family. I was disappointed when my paperwork specified I would be sent to Aliceville, Alabama, which was a 12-hour drive away from my family and friends. There is no guarantee that you will be designated close to your home. After I researched Aliceville, I discovered that it was a new prison, only two years old. Women from several other prisons had also been sent there to increase the headcount.

I was directed to report to Aliceville at 2pm on a Wednesday. My parents and I set out from Virginia on Tuesday, October 28, 2014, only ten months after I was initially charged. We spent the night in a Birmingham hotel which was an hour from Aliceville. I woke up at 5 am to pray. I prayed this situation was all a bad dream and I would awake from it. As I continued to meditate, the spirit of the Lord began to minister to me and I could sense the room was filled with His presence. I began to weep before the Lord and soon I was comforted again, by an unexplainable peace; the same peace that met me thirty days prior as I stood before the judge at my sentencing hearing. Amidst all the tears and shock of it all, I had been able to encourage my loved ones and assure them I would be ok. I just knew it. Now, here I was on the day I was scheduled to report, kneeling in the presence of God and trusting Him to go before me and protect me. Most importantly, I felt God had given me an assignment which would be revealed to me in due time after my arrival to prison.

As I sought God's direction that morning in Birmingham, I was determined to re-dedicate my life to Him and surrender my ALL to Him. By doing so, I set aside my own ideas and purposes, and chose to allow God to use me as a vessel to accomplish His will... even in prison. I resolved to be guided by Him and to represent His love to others. I would rely on God to show Himself to me in a grander way, being fully aware there would be a price to pay for His anointing on my life.

God will release his Spirit and anointing upon us as we trust and obey His promptings. Therefore, we are not able to pick or choose what He permits us to go through in life.

In my case, I believe prison was a part of my journey and a small price to pay for my disobedience towards God through remaining in relationship with one who God had warned me against. Although God's grace is sufficient for us, there are often consequences for our disobedience. I ignored my gut instincts and was blinded by deceit and lies. As a result, I endured verbal, emotional, and physical abuse at the hand of one whom I trusted. For seven years, I was under a spell of manipulation, control, and bondage disguised as ministry. I was truly lost and didn't realize it until I was empowered to be free. Only four years after my exit from the toxic relationship, I was charged as an accessory to his crime. When the Lord revealed to me my transgression, I repented and prayed that I would not have to go, but deep within me, I sensed that my purpose would be found within the walls of a federal prison.

It is difficult to describe my anticipation, knowing that God had something better in store for me and that my experience would be for His greater good. The experience has taught me that the things we go through are not always about us. I believe that many times God calls for us to comfort others and help to prevent them from repeating our mistakes. Haven't you ever prayed, "Lord, I want to be used by You! Lord, I'm available to You! Lord, I will surrender all to You!" If you have, prepare yourself to be used by God.

Believe it or not, the prison experience is an ideal training ground to birth the ministry that God has planted inside of you. It was *in prison*, where I learned to operate in the fruits of the spirit: love, joy, peace, patience, kindness, goodness, faithfulness, gentleness, and self-control. (Galatians 5:22-23). Prison is where I learned to 'let go and let God'—for REAL.

Our prison experiences are not intended to destroy us, but to thrust us into greater wisdom, to gain a better insight of our Heavenly Father's will for us. Therefore, try to look at your journey as a spiritual retreat or period of renewal with God. Enter your journey with a sincere heart and in anticipation of all that God has in store for your future.

***

Day 1

My parents and I arrived at the parking area at about 12:30 pm. I didn't worry, nor was I scared. In fact, I was very calm. About 30 minutes later, after all the tears had been shed, I indicated that I was ready to go inside. I did not allow my parents to go in with me; I felt that I needed to walk this path alone. As I set my feet in motion and moved towards the prison doors, I openly prayed these words, "Lord, I self-surrender to *You* and the purposes that You have for me at this place. Go before me and meet me on the inside. Dispatch angels of protection around me and give me favor with man. When people see me, let them see You. When people hear me, let them hear You. I go forth now in the power of Jesus Christ." I walked ahead never looking back at my parents. Armed with my bible, I walked into Aliceville Federal Correctional Institution.

An officer checked me in and led me to the Receiving and Departure (R&D) area. I was granted permission to bring in the following items: bible, my typed list of contacts, reading glasses, a necklace with a cross, and my $25 money order. I wore a pair of small silver hooped earrings. Other items that are permitted include: prescription eyeglasses, samples of your prescribed medication in the original bottles, a copy of medical records, a modest wedding band (no jewels).

What to wear: Don't buy a new outfit to go to prison. You will be provided with clothing—including undergarments. The things you wear to prison will be shipped home, unless you wish to 'donate' them. Don't be fooled, to donate means your items will likely be tossed in the trash. Don't wear makeup, nail polish, hair extensions (weave), artificial nails, lashes, or braids with additional hair.

Medication: You will not be permitted to have your medicine bottles. You will get generic prescriptions as substitutes for your pills, and you may not be given your meds for the first few days.

Intake process: This is an extremely *slow* process. You will have to meet with numerous individuals who will enter all your information into their systems. A nurse will ask general health questions and administer a Tuberculosis (TB) test, where a needle is placed just under the skin of your forearm. In three days, you must return to the nurse to check the results. You will also speak with a counselor who will ask about your current mental state and history. You will be strip searched. During the search, you must remove ALL clothing and you will be asked to 'squat, spread your cheeks, and cough.' An officer will visually investigate your private areas. This is quite degrading and dehumanizing.

I was given clothes to change into: sports bra, panties, socks, pants with an elastic waist band, a t-shirt, a short-sleeved button-down shirt and a pair of canvas slip on shoes. All laundered, but all USED. I asked for a sanitary napkin to line the crotch of the panties. Being in prison taught me to be resourceful and to think on my feet.

I was fingerprinted and had my picture taken for my badge, not my best photoshoot. After completing the booking process, my possessions were packaged to be sent to my home address. I was left in a holding cell with another young lady. Naturally, I was on edge after reading everything I could get my hands on regarding prison. Most of the information warned me against talking to anyone or disclosing personal information. I was uneasy being in an actual cell for the first time and I held my bible closely. My cellmate, Kristy, was on a furlough traveling from Waseca Prison. We engaged in small talk after establishing that we were both Christians and would most likely be housed together for a time. She became my 'prison tour guide' since I was unfamiliar with the process, and she had been incarcerated before. She gave me a crash course on what to expect every step of the way.

Although we were assigned to complete our sentences in prison camp, we were told that we would be in solitary confinement until beds were available. After being in the cell for approximately four hours, we were led to solitary and temporarily separated to be strip searched a second time and provided with a bright orange uniform with matching socks and shower shoes.

I was put in a tiny cell that had a stool fastened to the floor. It was clean. I still had my bible with me, so I read while I waited for whatever would happen next. I could hear Kristy calling out to me from another cell to ask if I was okay. About an hour later, we were handcuffed and moved to a secured area where other inmates were being held. As we were led past prison bars, faces stared at us from behind steel doors. We were instructed to enter the cell walking backwards, and the guard slammed and locked the door behind us. The small slot on the lower half of the door was unlocked and we were told to place our hands in the space so the handcuffs could be removed. It was the first time I had ever been handcuffed and the first of many days I would spend in prison.

Solitary confinement or 'Special Housing Unit'—known as 'The SHU'—is not 'special' at all. We were locked inside for 24 hours. We didn't know how long we would be in SHU, it depended on availability at the camp. While in SHU, we were not able to contact our families. One hour of recreation was given on Monday's but we arrived on a Wednesday, so we would be confined until the following week.

The 6' x 10' cell included a shower, toilet, desk, and a metal bunk bed bolted to the wall. We were given a thin mattress, 2 sheets, 2 flimsy blankets, 1 towel, 1 washcloth, 1 change of uniform, 1 pair of mesh underwear, and a pair of socks. We were also given a hygiene bag with 5 boxed sanitary napkins, a mini toothbrush designed to be used only with your thumb (if you can imagine that), a mini tube of toothpaste, 1 roll-on deodorant—both smaller than the average travel size—and shaving cream but no razor. Another packet contained four sheets of lined paper, a pencil, and two envelopes for letter writing.

After a quick assessment of our surroundings, Kristy and I began making our beds; well, Kristy actually had to make mine too, because I wasn't sure what to do with two top sheets and no fitted sheet. I was fascinated watching as Kristy covered the cushion with the first sheet, tying both ends with knots underneath to secure it. We agreed Kristy would get the bottom bunk due to her medical condition. I climbed up to the top using the two-step ladder attached to the bunk and spent the remainder of the day reading my bible and appreciating God for keeping me safe.

We could hear the guard's keys in the distance, which apparently meant dinner was on the way. The slot on the door was opened and Kristy was handed two covered trays. The food was actually pretty good my first night. I hated that we were given a powdered drink that had to be mixed with water from the sink on top of the toilet, but it was all we had. The lights were automatically shut off at 11 pm.

Each hour after lights out, the guards came to count us, shining their flashlights inside of each cell. To this day, I'm still haunted by the sound of the keys rattling and the crash of doors slamming each time they walked into the area. Amazingly, after finishing my prayers, I could sleep that night.

Lights came on at 5am and breakfast came at 6am. Trays were handed in through the slot in the door again for lunch and dinner. Kristy was sick from her bus trip, so she slept the whole day and didn't eat. After a shower, I continued reading and praying. I was so thankful to have my bible with me because reading comforted me and shifted my focus from where I was. There were screams coming from other cells and I could hear inmates conversing. Every sound in SHU was magnified. Even the toilets could be heard flushing. At one point, I came down from my bunk to look out the window on my door. The door was made of steel, and I had to stand on my tiptoes to see into the hallway. The windows were small but I could make out about 10 cells—five on each side directly across from the other. I saw the faces of the other ladies on the opposite side of the hall peeping out at me—young, old, white and black. Some were 'fishing' which I learned meant sliding notes and magazines under the door using the shower curtain or a pencil with string tied to the end. Others were yelling obscenities, trying to get the attention of the guards. After I'd had enough, I climbed back on my bunk and looked out another small window just below my head. Although, my view was just a barbed wire fence and spot lights, I quickly learned to appreciate the blue Alabama skies.

On day three, I began to get restless from being confined in such a small space. I woke up in the middle of the night after the lights were out. Turning my face to the wall, I prayed, appealing to God to intervene. I really did not know how much more of the screaming, key rattling, and toilet flushes I could take. My patience had worn thin and I felt trapped. Within a few hours my prayers had been answered. Shortly after breakfast, we heard a guard going to some of the cells and telling ladies to 'pack out.' Kristy and I were on that list and were told we were being released to the camp. Hearing the news, we embraced, jumping up and down like two school girls, all the while praising God. We were strip searched again (for the third time) and provided an army green uniform consisting of a button-down shirt with matching pants and navy canvas shoes. The officer handed me shoes that were two different shades of blue and told me to "deal with it."

Kristy and I were led inside a holding room with 12 other women who were also being released to the camp. We were all served lunch and had to wait until it was safe to move us to the next location. We were counted and handcuffed, then led to the security gate. Our last names were called and we each identified ourselves by inmate number. Once the last person was verified, we were un-cuffed and led out of the front door of the prison and told to walk the quarter mile towards the camp.

It was a taste of freedom and it seemed like we had been locked up for much longer than three days. I had never been so glad for sunshine and to feel the warm breeze blowing through my hair. It was a twenty-minute walk and we did not have an officer to escort us to the camp. It was surreal. We were not fenced in and we could see traffic passing on the main street. We walked slowly and laughed as we shared our SHU experiences. There were two ladies who, like me, were carrying bibles. We talked about how God kept us, and I learned that some had been in solitary for nearly three weeks waiting to be moved. Turns out that Kristy and I had spent the least amount of time in the SHU. Once again, God had shown me favor and confirmed that He was with me every step of the way.

Chapter 8

DIVINE CONNECTIONS

WHEN WE ARRIVED AT THE CAMP, we were directed to a tall wooden gate which separated the main office from the D and E housing units. An officer at the camp directed us to the laundry area where we were issued our uniforms and bedding. We were given 3 army green colored men's uniforms: 2 short-sleeved button-down shirts, 1 long sleeved button-down shirt, and 3 pairs of elastic waistband pants that were unfinished at the bottom so I had to cuff them. We got 3 pairs of new white sports bras, 3 pairs of new brown panties, and 3 pairs of new white socks. The rest of the girls were given steel toed work boots, but they were out of my size so I was told to keep the discolored canvas shoes which had holes underneath. We were also given a large mesh laundry bag with a drawstring that held 2 brown top sheets, 2 beige blankets, 2 thin bath towels and 2 washcloths. We also had an extra laundry bag and 2 hooks—one for white clothes and one for dark—that would be used to secure our clothes together on laundry days. Everyone's dirty clothes were tossed in a large bin and only identified by the hooks with your name written on them.

We were then directed to Unit E to see the counselor for our bed assignments. All fourteen of us were on display as 'new girls' as we headed 100 feet across the yard to Unit E. Once inside it was pure chaos as we were stared at, yelled at, and ridiculed. We were wearing used clothing that was too big, our hair was all over our heads, and we looked like we were lost. All of us except for Kristy were classified as first time, non-violent, white collar offenders. She was a repeat offender and was there on a gun charge, but was set to be released in a year. As we walked across the yard, Kristy saw several people she knew from other prisons. She introduced them to me and let them know that I was 'cool.' I followed her and we all went inside to see the unit counselor.

My first impression of the counselor was that she hated her job and didn't really want to deal with any of us. The process of assigning beds was confusing and unorganized. The counselor appeared to be overwhelmed that there were so many of us at one time. We could tell that she wasn't at all prepared for us. Twenty temporary bunks had recently been built in the common areas while we were in SHU which meant we were the overflow inmates. The common area was where inmates ate, played card games, watched television and had access to telephones and microwaves. It was by far the noisiest and most crowded place in the unit, but it was the only space available. We would have to wait for regular bunks one by one as other inmates were released, which was not that often.

An inmate who worked with the counselor dragged 14 brand new mattresses from a storage closet and placed them in the middle of the floor. We were given toilet paper, sanitary napkins and miniature hygiene items. As she called our names and gave us our bed number, we grabbed our mattress and left to find our bunk.

Only the elderly or persons with health issues received a special pass from the medical department and were assigned bottom bunks. All of us were assigned to D-Unit which was directly adjacent, separated only by a glass wall. The 'units' were basically identical, except E-Unit was cleaner and had air conditioning. I later learned that D-Unit was considered the 'projects,' and that most of the girls there were younger and known for causing trouble. I personally think that E-unit had a different vibe because the counselor and case manager occupied offices there during the day, and of course they were going to make sure that where they spent their time would be comfortable. E-Unit's inmates were also mostly long-timers, meaning that they had been in prison between 5 and 15 years and were pretty much on the tail end of their sentence. Some had become somewhat institutionalized and didn't have much patience for foolishness, so most of the short-timers were sent to D-unit where foolishness was in rare form most days.

Both D & E units held approximately 150 female inmates on each side. The unit itself looked like army barracks with bunk beds, and each 'room' was divided by two 8-foot metal lockers with an adjoining desk and 2 plastic chairs. There was no privacy. If you look to the left or right, you see straight down into the rooms of others on your aisle. Thankfully, the restrooms did have doors.

There were 12 stalls, six on each side divided by a wall with sinks attached. You had to bring your own toilet paper and hand soap, but there was a cabinet with a supply of tampons, razors, and toothpaste, to be used as needed. In the shower area, there were 16 individual showers with curtains. Four of them were handicapped showers with bars and a bench for some of the older inmates. There was a spray bottle and scrub brushes available to clean the shower before and after each use. They were also cleaned several times a day by unit orderlies, which was a plus. There were two TV rooms, the first had a news television and general viewing. The second room was for sports and Spanish viewing. There was also a 32-inch television in the common area on the wall. You could only listen to the TV if you had a radio or MP3 player.

Some of the ladies were nice enough to lend their players when they weren't using them. I was surprised at the generosity and kindness of most. Prison was nothing like I had imagined, and nothing like what I had seen on television. We also had a beauty room that had 2 shampoo bowls and chairs, and it was also equipped with curling irons and blow dryers. Next to that was a fitness room with a treadmill and exercise bikes. We also used this room to iron our uniforms. Along the wall in the common area were seven pay phones—three on one wall and four on another. Every day, those of us in the temporary bunks endured loud and personal phone conversations until nearly midnight when the phones shut off.

Kristy and I were assigned as bunkmates again which suited me fine. I had the top bunk which meant I could see my entire unit as well as most of E-Unit. Our bunk was right in front next to the aisle where most of the traffic was. We made our beds and tried to make the best of it despite all the noise. The common area was known as the 'bus stop' and the bright overhead lights stayed on all night. At the time, we didn't have any lockers to put our belongings in so we had to use cardboard boxes. Kristy's friends came by to bring her snacks that she shared with me. Once settled, I sat in a daze and observed my new surroundings, shaking my head in amazement. I could not believe that I was really in prison.

Several women came up front where we were to introduce themselves and offer snacks. I was surprised how genuine they seemed, but I was also guarded. I had heard so many horror stories and advice about not trusting anyone, not talking to anyone and not taking anything from anyone. They were asking where we were from. There was a group of us from Louisiana which prompted conversations to see if you were related or connected in any way. It was funny to see the reactions when someone realized that they knew the same people. Although I lived in Virginia, I was from Baton Rouge, and it was only a matter of time before I too would be quizzed.

One young lady, a few years older than me, was from Baton Rouge. She was going person to person asking where we were from. She was loud and persistent, but she looked like she could be in my family. I found out that she grew up in a small town where my great aunt and cousins resided. Soon we discovered that she did know quite a few of my relatives and she knew them by name. I felt comfortable talking to her and we continued to talk as she asked about several of my family members. It was not until she realized that she knew my father that her posture completely changed. She told me that she was good friends with my father and he had been kind to her on many occasions.

As if suddenly inspired, she told me to grab my empty laundry bag and follow her to her bunk. I did as I was told and when she opened her locker, it overflowed with commissary items. She pulled out various hygiene and food items and threw it on the bed and told me to put them in my bag. When I finished, I had shower shoes, t-shirts, lotion, and a comb and brush set. I even had cups, bowls, and eating utensils. I could not believe it. Everything was new and still in its package. When she filled up my bag, she had to help me carry it to my bunk. It amazed me! Earlier we were told that we would not be able to shop for commissary items until the following week, but God had sent me an angel on my first day and all my needs were met in that instant.

When I got back to the front area dragging that bag, all the ladies who arrived with me stared at me in shock. It was like we were all homeless and each of us would be grateful for any little thing. A few moments prior, I had known exactly what that felt like. So, I went in my bag and distributed items to each one of those ladies. I assured them that if I had, that they too would have. God had promised to supply all my needs and that simple gesture prompted the beginning of my ministry in prison.

Chapter 9

OBSERVING YOUR SURROUNDINGS

WHEN YOU FIRST GET TO A PRISON, it is wise to observe your surroundings and keep your conversation to a minimum. You are classified by your peers as soon as you step in the door. This does not mean that you should be rude or unfriendly, but there is no harm in keeping to yourself for the first few months before having a lot of interaction with others. You will be surprised at what you can learn about people when you observe their behavior and see how they interact with others. You will find out everything you need to know about an individual as well as your new environment if you simply tune in to what is going on. Most of the time, the person you meet on your first day will be totally different after sixty days. When housed together, the truth of a person is revealed in ways that would otherwise not be known. You learn personal habits and the authenticity of a person when you share a space.

Kristy and I developed a mutual respect. We shared the same space and she remained genuine to me until she left. She respected my choice to be alone and I respected her choice to be connected to her former friends. I spent most of my time on the top bunk reading and observing the environment when I wasn't walking on the track. I was cordial to everyone and I kept my conversation to a minimum. I politely excused myself from congregating groups and eventually gained a reputation as a Godly woman who was kind to everyone. Over time, I even developed a good rapport with the officers. Officers pay attention and can distinguish the good from the bad. It is possible to earn their respect by the way you act and by the way you treat others.

There are several types of people that can be easily identified in prison:

The Helper—This will be your go-to person in prison. They will give you the pre-orientation tour and make themselves available to assist you and answer any questions you may have. This person will usually have a good rapport and the respect of others in prison. They will freely provide you with any information or necessities with no strings attached. They genuinely just want to help. I was most definitely a helper.

The Interviewer—A very bold and direct personality when it comes to asking questions, they will attempt to pry into your personal business without hesitation. They may come off as cordial, but their main goal is to find out all they can about you so they can spread this information to others. News travels fast in prison, and you are the new person which makes you a target in many ways. The main things the interviewer will be interested in knowing are:

- Where are you from?
- How much time do you have?
- What are you in for?

A sure way to avoid this line of questioning without being rude is to use wisdom when providing your answers. For example, when asked where you are from, there is no harm in answering this question truthfully, because your state code will be the last 3 digits of your register number. Most inmates from similar areas will be familiar with the state codes and this information is not hard to find on your badge. When asked how much time I had, I found that the best way to respond was to say something like, "I have way more than I would like to have," or "I have a good bit of time." When asked what I was in for, my response was, "My case is still pending," or "I don't wish to discuss my case." Most people will get the hint and accept your answers. Remember, if you remain guarded, one can sense that you will not be open to disclosing your personal information.

The Con—This is a skilled manipulator who targets new inmates to get money or other items. They start by observing your behavior once you arrive in prison. They watch how you keep your space and your belongings. They will also monitor what you spend on commissary and how often you use the phone and email. When they have determined that you are not indigent, they will befriend you. Soon after, they will present a heartbreaking story about their children or about not having enough money to get basic necessities or food items. You can avoid this person by telling them a sob story of your own.

The Know It All—Hail the self-appointed authority on everything and everybody. They will try to tell you who you need to stay away from and what everyone is in prison for. They have been to other prisons and will always make comparisons. Stay clear of this person. They keep confusion going and are always in the middle of things. They spread tales, hide their hand, and are generally disruptive.

The Loner—Choosing to do their time alone with minimal associations, the loner seems unapproachable and is usually quiet and reserved. Often seen alone, usually reading or writing, they have limited interaction with others. This person does not get involved in the day-to-day drama and is respected by others. This person has proven to be trustworthy and is an advisor or confidante to many.

The Religious Fanatic—This is an overzealous person who professes Christianity but spends their time judging and criticizing others, rarely operating in Christ's unconditional love. Most likely they have been incarcerated for a long period of time, and now preach a prison gospel which is not truth. They will present themselves as an angel of light, but are very manipulative and controlling. They can be seen promoting gossip under the guise of prayer groups. Stay away from these groups! Ask the Lord to connect you with positive groups where you can receive legitimate support and healing.

The Jailhouse Lawyer—You'll find this person in the legal library researching criminal cases. They have gained a reputation for helping others file motions on their cases, or providing unsolicited legal advice. I must admit that all the advice is not necessarily bad or incorrect, but you must use wisdom. Be aware there are many cons in prison who 'practice law' as a means of support. In most instances, the jailhouse lawyer is committed to searching for loopholes within their own case that would lower their sentence. In the process, they have gained information that is valuable to others. I have witnessed several reductions in sentence based on the counsel of jail house lawyers. Though I would generally not advise one to disclose details of their case to others in prison, should you choose to go this route, make sure that you have observed the character of this person over time, and that you get proof of their results from an actual 'client.'

The Hustler—This is a jack-of-many-trades in prison. This person oversees an operation in prison that provides services for a fee. These services include: body massage, nails, hair, ironing, cooking, cleaning, laundry, party decorations, crocheting, stealing and even lying. Just about anything can be bought in prison.

The Bully—Just like in the schoolyard or the workplace, this is a person who taunts and harasses others for no reason. This person will cause disturbances within the housing unit by being loud and boisterous. Most often they will be controlling and confrontational, and will 'perform' when they can't have their way.

So again, it is best to take at least the first 30 days of your incarceration to observe your surroundings and the behavior of other inmates before forming associations and friendships. Many in prison are simply good people who made bad choices, and they just want to do their time and go home. Others are career criminals or malcontents who continue to make bad choices and use the prison system to their advantage.

Use your discernment and intuition to discover who is trustworthy before letting your guard down.

***

You will likely find the process of getting settled in prison to be very emotional and overwhelming. It may take days, weeks or even months for reality to set in and for you to really come to terms with the fact that you are actually in prison. For a while it was foreign to me and I simply could not wrap my mind around being incarcerated. My days were spent reading my bible. I was determined to seek God's purpose for my life while I was there. What had I missed seeing when I was in the free world? What was He trying to teach me? I decided I would use this time to somehow discover answers to my burning questions.

I explored the limited opportunities on the compound, and made up my mind to make the best of what Aliceville had to offer—which was not much. Since the prison was only a year old at the time, there were not many jobs or activities available. It was understaffed, and 90% of the time there was no supervision at the camp.

A GED program was the only class that was offered. Though there were several inmate-taught classes, such as crochet and yoga, there was no real rehabilitation taking place. Inmates were rarely even required to get out of bed in the morning.

For the first few weeks in prison, my conversation with others was limited and almost non-existent. I was cordial, but I did not reveal much about myself to others. Many will want to know about you and try to figure you out. You will be in a vulnerable state and will probably want to share your feelings with those you feel you can relate to. You may want to vent. Some will put on their best faces to get information from you that will only circulate throughout the camp. Only share what you don't mind others knowing. Do not discuss details about your case or how much time you have been required to serve.

There were some individuals that I shared with because they initially shared details of their own situations, and I felt comfortable sharing some of mine. In hindsight, I would have not been as transparent. Trust me, as time goes on you will see people for who they really are and you will regret sharing your information. The person you meet at first may change over time.

In prison, initially some people will not show you their authentic self. You must take time to observe them and their spiritual walk with God. Pay attention to how they spend their time. Just because they carry a bible does not mean they read it or believe it. The bible says, *you should know them by their fruit.* Do they have fruitful conversation or do they gossip about others? Do they participate in fruitful activities or are they engaged in negative behavior? Pay attention. Don't let your days be filled with unfruitful activities. Spend the first few minutes of each day with God in prayer and reading scripture. Quiet time in the presence of God sets the foundation for a dedicated and committed life honoring the Father. Plan time to spend with God or you will find yourself lost and doing other things. Start small. Read at least one scripture a day and spend 3 minutes in communication and prayer. Each day increase the number of scriptures and add two minutes of prayer. Seek God's guidance for preparing your heart and mind to hear Him. Begin to thank Him for each new day. Ask Him to quiet your mind so that you can hear Him. As you sit quietly in His presence, allow Him to speak to your heart.

Stay away from the 'noise.'

Chapter 10

FAMILY TIES

ONE VERY HARD REALITY FOR ME once I entered prison was the lack of consistent support from my loved ones. Prior to going away, I made the difficult decision to not disclose details to my family in Louisiana, except for my biological father. My other family members and I had grown distant, and I rarely spoke with them unless we were at a family function, plus I didn't need all the extra drama that news of my ordeal would bring.

Once I decided to take the plea deal, I was instructed by the prosecuting attorney to return to Virginia to voluntarily surrender to the court and to attend my initial appearance and plea hearing. Since I lived out of state, my attorney arranged for me to have both hearings on the same day. The first hearing was painless as the judge advised me of my charge and the maximum penalty it carried. At the end of the hearing, I was taken to the processing area to be photographed, fingerprinted and officially entered into the 'system.' I was not handcuffed and my attorney remained with me. Afterwards, I returned to the courtroom for my next hearing.

Honestly, this was all quite overwhelming for me. I stood before the judge as he went over details of my plea agreement to make sure I understood what I was agreeing to. I was terrified. I didn't know what any of the legal jargon meant, and I no longer had much trust in my attorney. I had to trust only God to see me through.

I was reluctant to sign the agreement drafted by the prosecutor because my attorney had failed to challenge some items on my behalf as I had requested. After a five-minute recess that included a sixty second meltdown and a pep talk from my lawyer, I again stood before the judge and signed the agreement. I was scheduled to return for sentencing in ninety days and left the courtroom that day… a convicted felon.

I returned to Louisiana and went to work the next day, trying my best to act as normally as possible. By the end of the day, my job had been notified of my new criminal record and I was immediately let go. Thankfully, I had a great supervisor who spared me the embarrassment of alerting my co-workers, and allowed me to leave with some sense of dignity. So far, it was the worse day of my life, but a part of me was relieved. I had been wearing a mask and carrying this heavy burden for nearly six months. I was exhausted, and at that point just wanted it all to be over. I suffered alone; with no friends, and no family. I considered taking my life that day... but God stood with me.

I had true friends who meant more to me than family, but they were in Virginia. I called them one by one and told them I had lost my job. They had attended court with me a few days prior and were aware of what I was facing. By the weekend, they were on a plane to comfort me. When they arrived, we went and traveled to Pensacola Beach which was a 4-hour drive. They cried with me, prayed with me, and ultimately helped me get myself together. My friends, who I consider sisters, assured me I would not have to take this journey alone, and that they would be with me every step of the way. Because of my fragile state, they insisted I return to Virginia with them. It was a no-brainer for me. A month later, I had ended my apartment lease agreement and said goodbye to Louisiana.

When the news of my ordeal finally reached my family in Louisiana, I had already been sentenced and was scheduled to surrender to prison within thirty days. As expected, drama ensued. There were tears and phone calls, and of course no shortage of family gossip. Everyone wanted to know why I didn't tell them what was going on. Seriously? I knew they would judge me based on the news report. It's just who they are, and unfortunately, what they do. Still, I craved any amount of concern and compassion I could get from my family. My reality was coming in just a few days, and life as I had known it would end. I didn't have time to be concerned about what others felt or thought about me, but I had really hoped they would be there for me when I needed them most. Boy, was I ever disappointed.

I was designated to a site only five hours away from my family in Louisiana. In the thirteen months I was incarcerated, I was heartbroken when only my father took the time to visit me. Not one person sent me money to help sustain me. Imagine how devastated I felt to learn of family trips that extended past or near my location.

I am grateful for the few cards I received during my first month, but I felt like they were "pity" cards. If you can accept this truth, it will save you some heartbreak: your incarceration may well end up being more uncomfortable for others than for you. Some won't know how to deal with it, so they will avoid you and the situation entirely. Yes, you will be disappointed by the absence of your family and friends while you are away, so try to prepare for this ahead of time. Try not to have unrealistic expectations of them. Your incarceration will teach you a lot about people and what they deem important or necessary. It is a good lesson to learn. Ask yourself this honest question as you consider these issues: *Could I depend on this person to help me before I was sent to prison?* If you answered no, then you'll only set yourself up for disappointment if you depend on them to show support while you are there.

People generally do the things they want to do, and make excuses for those they don't want to do. It's not personal... yet it IS personal when you're the one sitting in prison with no support. I describe prison as a kind of death experience, yet you go through it while you live. The reality is, life continues to go on for others while you are away. Don't allow bitterness and unforgiveness to take root in your heart over it.

Maintain consistent contact with those who are willing, through visitation, phone calls, video chat, emails, and letters, as often as possible. There are many options, but it can become expensive to utilize all of them. Do what works for you. Don't be afraid to ask for help for your children. There are many programs that provide support for the children of inmates, especially during the holiday season.

Here are a few ways to show your support for a friend or family member who is incarcerated:

1) Purchase a few boxes of assorted blank cards and a book of stamps. They can be found for about $2 at Walmart or even a dollar store. In your spare time, write notes of encouragement in each card. It can be a poem or something inspiring that you find online. Pick a day of every week to mail one card to your

loved one in prison. It only takes a few minutes and it will be the highlight of the recipient's day. It will lift them up each time it arrives, and once a pattern is established, give them something to look forward to. This is the best thing you can do for someone who is incarcerated.

2) Put money on the books for your loved one. It doesn't have to be a lot of money, and anything would help. Even as little as $20 a month would be very helpful. There are items available through the commissary more nutritious than the meals served from the kitchen. Your loved one will appreciate your help as often as you can assist them, and a little goes a long way.

3) If possible, schedule to visit your loved one as often as you can. Often, inmates opt not to have visitation so they can avoid the dehumanizing process of strip searching. This is understandable, however, your loved one needs interaction from those who are on the outside as often as possible.

4) Purchase a magazine or newspaper subscription to be forwarded to your loved one. Most facilities have no real programs to offer. Your loved one will need reading material to keep their mind stimulated so they don't resort to reading only what the prison library offers.

5) Send current pictures. Your loved one will be excited to have personal effects that remind them of home.

6) Help your loved one's child create drawings and cards for their parent who is incarcerated.

7) Email and video chat as often as possible.

My best friend, who is more like a sister to me, made sure that I had *everything* I needed when I was in prison. Every time I called, she answered. When I emailed, she responded. Whatever I asked for, she sent it to me—books, letters, cards, money, whatever it was, she did not miss a beat. She was my lifeline, and I pray that everyone has at least one person in their life who is equally as devoted. It really makes a difference in how you get through a prison experience.

Remember your loved ones do the time with you, and that your incarceration affects everyone in your life who cares for you. Some will handle the news of your situation better than others. Again, be careful not to allow bitterness and unforgiveness to take root in you. It will be easy to hold a grudge, but take it to the Lord in prayer and allow him to heal your heart and your hurts.

Chapter 11

DOING TIME

THE FACILITY IN ALICEVILLE WAS only about a year old when I arrived. Because it was new, many women had been moved from other prisons to increase the headcount. There were very few programs established and even fewer job opportunities. My first thirty days were very challenging. We were not required to do anything. We didn't even have to get out of bed if we didn't want to. My days were spent either walking on the track or sitting in the chapel library.

Each prison should have a law library, general library, and chapel library. The law library may be used for inmates who research case law. A typewriter is available for those who prepare legal documents for themselves or for other inmates. The general library houses books, magazines, and newspapers that have been donated by inmates. You may also find self-help books and independent study material such as foreign language audio and video tapes. There may even be some educational materials. The donated books come in all genres, but I saw mostly urban, erotic, and mystery books. I preferred the chapel library where I could find inspirational books and novels, as well as Christian DVD's that I could watch if I had headphones. It was the quietest area on the compound.

Next to the library was the room that was used as the chapel. Each denomination had a designated time to have their religious services, but the chapel could also be used for prayer whenever a service was not in session. In the same building were classrooms. The only classes taught at the time were GED and English as a Second Language, and both were taught by inmates. After my first six months there, additional classes were added, but none I could really benefit from. There was GED preparation, Egyptian Studies, Crocheting, Scrapbooking, Drumming, and Yoga.

The handbook and website may outline other educational programs, but most likely it will not be accurate. Inmates who were experts in their professions made requests for materials to introduce new courses and programs, but they had very limited teaching materials. They would have to be resourceful and get a loved one to email or mail materials. I had to discover my own ways to stimulate my mind and occupy my time… by reading and writing.

There were limited jobs available too, and included: unit orderly, laundry, kitchen, haircare, grounds keeping, library and commissary. The orderlies were responsible for keeping the housing units clean. This included the bathrooms, showers, and common areas. There were about ten people who rotated as orderlies. Laundry duties consisted of taking laundry carts to the higher-level security section of the prison complex to be washed and dried. The clothes were returned in the evening on the designated days. Laundry workers also distributed clean sheets and blankets to inmates once a month. Kitchen workers were responsible for preparing and serving meals at the prison. The three shifts included breakfast at 6am, lunch at noon, and dinner at 5pm. Grounds keepers were responsible for the lawn care and overall upkeep of the grounds. Haircare workers were licensed stylists who operated the hair salon. It was just like a real beauty salon with shampoo bowls, hair dryers, curling irons, and hair color. After ninety days, I was blessed to be able to work in haircare after one of the two stylists was transferred out. Haircare and commissary positions were the highest paid in the prison. I made a whopping 12 cents an hour, compared to others who only made 12 cents per day.

Commissary workers operated the prison store once a week. Every other job was monitored by an officer, except mine. I established a favorable rapport with the guards and gained their respect. So, they only came to haircare to open and lock up at the end of the day. It was my prison dream job, and became my sanctuary. It was the closest thing to being in the outside world for me. I could schedule my own hours and come to the salon whenever I wanted. The other stylist and I became fast friends and worked around each other's schedules. I made sure to have many customers and long hours, because it made my days go faster—and there were some LONG days. It was God who miraculously opened that door for me. I didn't go out seeking the position, I was recommended for it. God will provide all that you need to sustain you—if only you just trust in Him.

When I wasn't in the salon, I was trying to find ways to pass the time. If I was in the housing unit, my face was in a book reading or else I was writing. I had to learn how to make the best use of my time. Inmates are required to participate in development courses, and meet with the case manager every six months for what is known as Program Review. Your case manager will document your efforts to promote self-improvement. Unfortunately, prison is a setup for failure in the real world, so your resources will most likely be limited. You may even have to develop your own creative methods to meet the requirements for rehabilitation.

Here are some suggestions for self-development:

1) Write to churches that offer correspondence bible studies. This will require you to purchase postage. You will be mailed a new lesson each time one is completed and returned. After all lessons have been completed, you will be mailed a certificate. These certificates will be considered acceptable documentation at your review. By the time I left prison, I had completed fifty or more lessons.

2) If possible, enroll in a correspondence course. Have a loved one research college courses or certificate programs that cater to incarcerated individuals. The school will mail you any required materials or textbooks. There may be a cost to participate in these programs. I enrolled in a Paralegal Certification course. It is a self-paced program that can be completed in 3-9 months depending on the individual. Your participation in these courses will be favorable on your review.

3) You can also write to churches to request a bible be sent to you. There are some ministries who will adopt an inmate to send donations to.

4) Some prisons will allow ministries from local colleges to teach courses at the prison. You should register for these classes also. Not only will you

receive college credit, but most will issue a certificate of completion.

5) Try to participate in group discussions or workshops that are facilitated by outside organizations. Usually they are about 4-6 weeks long. Certificates are issued when the class ends.

6) Start a journal and document your experience. Writing a book can be very therapeutic and could also prove to be lucrative after your release from prison.

7) Request study materials and/or worksheets to be mailed to you. There are many ways to keep your mind stimulated, and completion of workbooks will be considered self-improvement at your program review.

8) Use your expertise to help others. Don't be afraid to create programs to assist others who are incarcerated. In some instances, these programs will be approved by the warden.

9) Build rapport with those in authority. Someone is always watching you. Maintain a good attitude and treat everyone with respect. Opportunities may arise when you need someone in authority to support your program and speak on your behalf.

***

Once I adapted to my environment and concluded there was not much to do to occupy my time, I started a weekly discussion group with the ladies I came from SHU with. We met every week to encourage one another as we adjusted to prison life. We connected in prayer for our families and loved ones, and we kept each other motivated.

Utilizing my position in haircare, I asked my customers to donate items for new inmates. Soon, I had a collection of hygiene products and other items available. Inmates arrived every Wednesday before the 4pm count time. I greeted them at the door and delivered items to them. This created a chain reaction from other inmates. Naturally, new ladies were apprehensive about receiving items from others, so I had to assure them there was no ulterior motive, we were simply paying it forward. I can't tell you how many times those who had nothing would break down and cry over receiving those items.

When you enter prison, it can take a few days before you gain phone privileges, have access to email, or are able to purchase commissary items. My 'welcome' bags had a notebook and pen, stamps, envelopes, a cup, plate and fork, and a variety of name brand, full size, hygiene products and shower shoes. All donated by other inmates.

Another way I chose to occupy my time was by assisting others. There was a 'whosoever will, let them come' choir that sang at the weekly church services. Some of the ladies wanted to do solo's but lacked confidence. Not that I consider myself to be a great singer, but I have had experience in church choirs and could identify singing parts. A few ladies heard me sing and asked if I would give voice lessons. The word spread, and the next thing I know, I was doing vocal coaching, and lessons on praise and worship. I wrote home and asked the praise leader at my church to send me the lessons she used in her workshops. When I received the lessons, God opened the opportunity and I allowed Him to use me to share with them. They trusted me and followed my instruction. I would smile as I passed ladies doing vocal exercises throughout the day. They could even be heard practicing in the shower.

This opened another opportunity for me. I was approached by another inmate who had spoken to some of my vocal students. She wanted to start a singing group with more experienced singers. I was happy to support anything positive and to be an encouragement to those utilizing their gifts to help others. This young lady was Muslim, but I think she may have grown up Christian and later converted. Anyway, she loved gospel music and so did I. She recruited a few others and we were a group. We had regular rehearsals in one of the recreation rooms. Soon spectators formed outside of the door to hear us rehearse, and I must admit, we were good.

Sadly, our group was not permitted to sing at the Sunday services because our leader was Muslim. We were told by the Chaplain that the religions could not be combined for service and that Muslims had to attend their own designated services. It was the craziest thing I had ever heard of. This is just one of many roadblocks meant to deter your growth in prison. The system is designed to frustrate your growth, but you must see obstacles and overcome them. Discovering opportunities to help others is the best way to pass the time.

Of course, working in haircare provided endless opportunities for me to counsel and minister the Word of God to my peers. I was a loyal confidante and took their concerns to God in prayer. The salon was a 'no judgement zone' and the ladies could be transparent with me. I learned that some were 'gay for the stay,' as the saying goes—living homosexual lives only while in prison. Some had husbands and children who were not aware of this temporary lifestyle. Although, I may not have understood the reasoning behind their choices, I chose to simply be an agent of God's love and remain available to them as often as needed. I would continue to lift them up and pray for them and allow Him to draw them. I understood my assignment was to plant seeds and trust God to send others to water those seeds while He determined the increase. (1 Corinthians 3:6) As a result, souls were saved and hearts were healed, right there in Aliceville haircare.

It wasn't easy in prison by any means, and I could not have made it without a relationship with God. There were bad days and it was easy to give up and give in to depression. I watched people stay in bed all day for weeks at a time. The officers weren't always nice, and some of the inmates were disrespectful. However, once you pray and ask God to reveal your assignment to you, it will become your focus. You will discover ways to make the system work for you, and God will help as you trust His leading. He will help you to identify needs that He has gifted you to meet. You will discover your purpose for being where you are, and God will get the glory from your experience.

Chapter 12

ON THE MOVE

AFTER MY SENTENCING, I HIRED a new attorney. I was not pleased with the performance of my first attorney and had ignored the red flags and suspected errors with the handling of my case. My worst fears were realized when my new attorney shared information with me that could have possibly changed my outcome and decreased my prison time. Once I began my prison sentence, my new attorney continued to work to get a court hearing that would get my sentence modified.

Approximately six months into my sentence, my new attorney informed me I would have to travel from Alabama to Virginia for the hearing. Due to extreme security measures that must be taken with inmates, he could not provide me with the date for the hearing, so I just had to wait until I was scheduled to be moved. He told me the journey would be a difficult one, but nothing could have prepared me for the actual experience. Although I prepared myself both mentally and spiritually—with prayer and daily scripture readings, it was still by far *the worst* experience of my life.

So, nine months into my sentence, I was awakened at 6 am by an officer. She was one of the good ones who treated us with respect. Since I slept with headphones in my ears and my head covered, she had to shake me a little. She told me to get dressed, pack up everything in my locker, and take my belongings to the main prison. She was very discreet as not to alert the other inmates. I showered and begin to pack my things as I was told. By this time, the word had travelled throughout my unit that I was leaving to go home. I had spoken this in faith to some and we were all hoping this was the case. There were hugs and tears all around. Many ladies ran to my area, some to wish me well, and some to ask for things or to just see what was going on. I gave most of everything away except for my personal books or study materials. I gave away food, clothes, hair products, magazines, most anything else I had that they wanted.

My personal belongings were labeled and stored in the Receiving and Departure department. The officer told me if I did not return to Aliceville, my property would be shipped to me. I was stripped searched and was given a short-sleeved khaki shirt and pants in exchange for the army green camp uniform. My boots were replaced with a disposable pair of thin Styrofoam-type slip-ons. I was placed in a holding cell alone and watched as twenty-nine other ladies from the higher security level prison were brought in and taken to the strip search area to change. They could not be placed in the same cell with me, because I was from the camp and had to be kept separate. I could hear them talking in their cell and they assumed I was separated because I was a maximum-security inmate, and therefore a danger to them. They didn't know I was from the camp, and I wasn't going to reveal anything about myself to them. I had been warned by my attorney to keep my conversation to a minimum during transport.

After about eight hours of waiting in the cell, two Federal Marshals arrived and we were handcuffed and put in shackles. It was a humiliating process and the Marshals were mean. One was holding a stack of folders; one for each of us. We were identified by our register number and photos on the front of the folders and told to line up when our number was called. It was difficult to walk with the shackles on. They were very tight, and the hard metal rubbed against the back part of my foot with those paper shoes on. The cuffs were also tight and locked in the middle, so my hands had to be held together in front of me. When everyone was accounted for, we were led outside to a large bus that resembled a charter bus. It was high off the ground with dark tinted windows, and I noticed there were armed officers standing around as we were boarding the bus. There were only two Marshals sent to transport us, the driver and his partner, who were also armed.

The officers at the camp hadn't carried weapons, so I was not used to seeing this. The seats on the bus were hard, plastic chairs, like in an elementary school. When we were all seated, we were locked in a cage. No one sat by me, which I was glad of, and appreciated having two seats to myself.

The ride lasted another eight hours. We were not told where we were going. We made periodic stops so the officers could go to the restroom and buy food. We were given a brown bag lunch with a bologna sandwich, an apple, and a small drink. We also had a lavatory at the back of the bus. When the door opened, the stench was enough to knock you off your feet. Luckily, I was seated near the front and did not have to deal with it too often.

The ride was very uncomfortable and most of us were restless and tired since we had been up since early that morning. I found myself constantly fidgeting to get relief for my back which ached from the hard seats. Some of the others laid on the floor in the isle of the bus. It was unnatural the way they were piled on the floor on top of each other like fallen dominoes. I tried my best to find a comfortable position leaned up against the window, but it was a challenge with my hands and feet secured. To add insult to injury, the marshals ridiculed and made fun of us.

We arrived at Lovejoy, Georgia at approximately 10 pm. We finally exited the bus and thankfully, our handcuffs and shackles were removed. The cuffs had cut into my wrists during the trip and my ankles were sore. We were placed in a room and given another brown bag lunch, and a water cooler was provided. There was trash and dirt on the floor and a bench that went around the perimeter of the space. It also had a toilet in the corner that was out in the open. Girls began to line up for the toilet, because most of us did not go on the bus if we could help it. Two girls would block the view while each person relieved themselves. I was grateful for those who stood for me.

There was a sink with no soap or paper towels. Thankfully, they had given us toilet paper. There was a television on the wall with no audio, but the closed captioning was turned on. One of the officers rolled in a payphone we could use. Next, the girls stood in line for the phone. The phone allowed you a free two-minute collect call, but the other party had to set up a phone account to receive follow-up calls. Prior to leaving Aliceville, I had asked my prayer partner to contact my mother, informing her of my departure. I did not have any details of this journey and did not know how long it would take. I was happy now to be able to call my parents and let them know I was in Georgia.

We were going to be in the holding room for a while because everyone had to be 'processed' before being assigned a bed. Processing included a strip search, a photo id badge, and medical and psychological evaluations. During the strip search, we were given a *clean* bright orange uniform and new underwear, socks, and canvas shoes. Our travel clothes were put in a bag, labeled, and stored. We were given another bag with a sheet, blanket, and two additional change of clothes, which included an orange sweatshirt, shower shoes, and t-shirt nightgown. I was pleasantly surprised that all of the items were laundered and smelled fresh, and some were brand new, which I really appreciated.

As it got later into the night, we each were given a mattress. Many of the girls secured a space on the floor. I opted to use the bench, which was just wide enough for the flimsy mattress. I used my bag of clothing for a pillow, but I simply could not go to sleep with all those women. They knew each other, but they were strangers to me.

At around 3am, the last group of girls had been processed and we were lined up with our belongings. We were led to the area where we would reside until we left. We were divided into groups and taken to our designated pod. It was dark and I was tired, so I couldn't really assess the environment at that time. I remember the officer shining the flashlight on the door that was my cell. When I entered, it was small with just a bunk bed and toilet. There was someone in the bottom bunk and she began to use profanity about the noise when I entered. I ignored her and tried to figure out how to make my bed and get on the top bunk without disturbing her. The lights were off, but I could see a little from an outside light coming through a small window above my bunk. I heard the steel door lock and realized I was locked in with a stranger. Somehow, I managed to maneuver my bedding in the dark without waking my cellmate. I was exhausted and didn't have the energy to obsess over whether I would be safe with her or not. I began to pray until my anxiety subsided. I knew I had to trust God to protect me while I slept in this unknown place and eventually I drifted off to sleep in peace.

I was awakened by the sound of someone yelling 'trays,' meaning breakfast had arrived. I heard the click of the door being unlocked and heard my cell mate leave out. A few minutes later, an officer stood at the door and called me by name. She addressed me as 'Miss Trudi' and asked me if I would be coming out to eat. I was taken aback by her kindness, and told her I would not be coming out. She asked me if I was okay, and I replied, *"Yes ma'am."*

I sat up and began to take inventory of my new environment. There was a desk, a shelf, a toilet and a sink in the room. A small plexiglass mirror hung over the sink. My cell mate had a few toiletries on the shelf and books on the desk and… a bible. I also noticed she had a small collection of mystery books and some that were inspirational. I smiled on the inside at the thought of having another divine assignment.

When she came in, I was looking out the window. Not much of a view, but I was able to see cars passing in the distance. She introduced herself and apologized to me for her outburst the night before. We engaged in small talk about the facility and she filled me in on how things worked there. My only concern at the moment was taking a shower. Our little chat would have to wait until later. She told me it would be best to wear the t-shirt gown into and out of the shower since there was not space for extra items. The shower was very clean and I could smell the bleach which was refreshing.

The pod itself was an open space with cells on one wall. There were six two-person rooms upstairs and another six downstairs. Each floor had its own shower at the corner of the room. There were two televisions and four telephones lined along another wall. A female officer was in the pod documenting each inmate's activities throughout the day. Overlooking the pod behind a tinted glass were other officers who monitored us and controlled the opening and closing of the cell doors. I was grateful to be in a safe and controlled environment.

After my shower, my cell mate and I resumed our conversation. She was a Christian and we clicked instantly after realizing we had our faith in common. She shared her story with me. She was a state inmate who had already served over six months on a drug charge. She talked about her children and her desire to be a better parent when she got out. She was fifteen years younger than me and spoke passionately about her need for direction and guidance. I took time to encourage her and we talked about the love of Jesus and how His grace and mercy had allowed us to endure the hard times in life and during incarceration. She offered me her bible and other inspirational books to read. She even sought out reading material from others that she thought would interest me. I spent the first several days in the cell fasting and in prayer, only coming out to shower and use the phone. I did not interact with the other inmates at first, but I was always polite when addressed.

After the first week, not knowing when we would leave, I purchased some hygiene products and food items from the commissary. A few days after receiving my things, I was awakened in the middle of the night and told to pack up my bedding. I was not allowed to take any of my purchases with me, so I left them for my cellmate. I was deeply moved by her tearful gratitude. It was the least I could do in response to her generosity during my stay. She had offered what little she had to help me when I arrived, so this was the least I could do.

Me and the twenty-nine others from Aliceville were again handcuffed, shackled and loaded onto a bus. This time, about twenty men were already on board as well. They yelled compliments and obscenities at us as we boarded. A cage separated the men from the women, and the women from the armed marshals. Some of the girls changed seats with others to get closer to the men. I was disgusted by those who were performing sexual favors on one another through the cage. Some of the girls reasoned they would be in prison for a long time and needed to have the touch of a man one last time. It was becoming a chaotic scene as most of the girls shuffled by to get her turn. I faced forward and ignored the cheers and loud outbursts. I was saddened at how the girls were disrespecting themselves with strangers, and wondered what had happened in their lives to give them such poor judgement. The marshals looked into the cage to investigate, but failed to intervene and put a stop to the madness.

After approximately an hour, we arrived behind the Atlanta airport. There were other unmarked, full-sized buses parked side by side. What seemed like hours passed before we headed to a secured area on the tarmac. Each bus was unloaded and the inmates were lined up. The men were gathered on one side and women on the other to be counted. There were armed marshals with loaded weapons aimed at us, and more marshals surrounded the outside of a large airplane. I realized we were going to board the plane next. I couldn't believe Con-Air was actually a real 'thing' and not just a movie like I once thought. Although, like a horrifying scene like out of the movie, the real thing is much more terrifying. Assault rifles were pointed at us and we were yanked and pushed around by armed bullies. They patted us down one by one and our handcuffs and shackles were tightened. I didn't think mine could get any tighter, but I was wrong. They were so tight now, I couldn't move my wrist without cutting myself. The male inmates continued to whistle and cat-call at us from all directions. I observed my surroundings and tried to capture each moment to document later, but it was hard to fathom this was actually happening to me.

The men boarded the plane first, and more boarded after we were seated. There were twelve women who boarded the plane with me. We were told not to look at or speak to the men, but they were winking and blowing kisses at us as they passed our seats. The only way to avoid it would have been to close my eyes, but I was curious. Naturally, some of the girls enjoyed the attention and winked back.

Lastly, the maximum-security inmates boarded the plane. I could tell by the locked black boxes connected to their handcuffs that these were the worst of the bunch. Some had tattoos that covered their entire faces. I didn't want to look at them, but there was quite a commotion getting some of them to cooperate. We were seated in the front of the plane, behind what would be the first-class section, but without the dividing curtain or separation. The rows had three seats on each side. The plane was huge and I counted twenty (yes, 20) armed marshals stationed in different sections.

It was the longest flight of my entire life, and all I could do was pray for God's protection. I did not know where I was going or what else to expect. I was terrified, but I trusted God would keep me safe. Before departing, we were given another dry bologna sandwich to eat, though I gave mine away. I had grown tired of those bag lunches. During the flight, the air conditioning was set on high and many inmates complained of being cold. It wasn't just cold, it was freezing! Most of us only had on a short sleeved uniform shirt with a t-shirt underneath. Men and women alike began to huddle together without shame, just to try and stay warm. Of course, the marshals had come prepared with jackets and skull caps. They had no mercy for us, and they laughed and took pictures of us with their cell phones. It was humiliating.

When the plane landed, we were not allowed to lift the window shades and they wouldn't tell us where we were. My name was called to exit the plane, and I heard one of the officers say we were in Philadelphia. Outside of the plane was the same thing I witnessed in Georgia—armed marshals circling the plane, weapons aimed, more busses and long lines of detained inmates.

My identity was verified and I was told to go to the back of a small bus and I was locked in a cage alone. A few minutes later, twelve African-American and three white male inmates also boarded the bus. Some began to call out to me to try and get my attention. I ignored them and continued to look out of the window with no visible reaction. I was not able to keep my hair tie, so all my hair was loose and hanging down. Due to my creole roots, I have been told that I look like I could be of Dominican descent. Fortunately, this played in my favor, as after not responding for a bit, the men concluded I didn't understand English. After a few more moments of me not responding to their calls, they finally gave up and ignored me.

Before leaving the airport, one of the marshals brought yet another sandwich in a brown paper bag. He asked if I needed to use the restroom, and I nodded in response. We were driven to a nearby location outside of the airport and parked in front of a portable toilet. I had to leave the cage to exit the bus, which meant walking by all the men. Although, we were still handcuffed and shackled, some of them used the opportunity to lean into the isle to rub up against me as I passed. Once I exited the bus, the respectful male officer asked if I was okay. I nodded and tried to hold back my tears. He un-cuffed me and I entered the stall. My wrists ached from the cuffs, and it was a relief to have them off, even for a few moments. The brief time alone in the stall was enough for me to center myself and say a short prayer for strength to get through the next stage of this horrific journey. I exited and looked around, spotting the waiting buses as my cuffs were put back on. Thankfully, the officer did not tighten them as much as before. I silently acknowledged my appreciation to him before re-boarding the bus. I walked hurriedly past the men and was locked back in the cage. The men were also allowed to use the stall once I was secured, and I noticed they remained handcuffed all the while.

We left the airport and travelled toward 95 South. I assumed we were heading to Virginia, and had heard some of the men say they hoped we were not going to Northern Neck Regional Jail. They described how awful the conditions were, and I found myself hoping we weren't going there as well. I listened to their conversations, but kept looking out the window. By the time we arrived four hours later, I had a headache from staring at trees for the whole duration of the ride. I could feel a few of them periodically looking back at me, but I refused to look in their direction. Soon, it got dark and I think they eventually forgot I was there.

As we got closer to our destination, I heard a few of the men confirm we were going to Northern Neck. They recognized a few landmarks and again expressed displeasure at our destination. They talked about the horrible food and the overall poor condition of the jail. I could not imagine this and had nothing to compare it to. Fortunately, I had been housed in fairly good conditions up to this point, and Lovejoy was better than Aliceville in terms of cleanliness. I could not imagine it being *that* bad… but I was soon to discover it was.

The van entered a dark garage behind the jail and we were unloaded. This time, I was last to get off. The men were lined up, un-cuffed and grouped into various holding cells. It was the first time I had seen actual cells with bars. I was led into the jail where my cuffs and shackles were removed. Once again, the men began yelling to get my attention, but I ignored them. My cuffs were removed and I was placed into a cell with another woman.

The cell was so repulsive, I didn't want to touch anything. There was a rusty toilet in the corner that appeared to not have been cleaned since God only knows when. Up against the wall was a steel bunk with no mattress on it. The woman had on street clothes and reported she was there for driving with a suspended license. She did not ask me any questions and I was not feeling cordial at this point. I'd been on a trip from hell and it was getting worse by the second. I couldn't begin to determine when the last time this place had been cleaned.

After careful inspection, I reluctantly sat on the edge of the metal bunk. After a few minutes, the young white woman—of about thirty—was removed from the cell, and I remained alone. I could hear the men talking in cells all around me, and someone in the next cell passed a note to me on the floor. I ignored it—and the man who sent it—as he tried to get my attention. I sat on the empty bunk with my arms wrapped around my knees and looked around the cell. There was splattered blood on the ceiling and what appeared to be feces on the wall. It was nauseating.

I watched from my cell as each of the men who had arrived with me were processed and returned to their cells. This booking process consisted of being photographed and asked a series of questions. Each person also was required to watch a video on sexual harassment. Afterwards, I saw them go into a room and be given a change of clothing. Moments later, each inmate re-appeared with a navy-blue uniform that had the name of the jail on the back.

Soon after, an officer came around to deliver dinner trays on a rolling cart. The food was unrecognizable and I quickly declined my meal. I continued to watch as several men were given a mattress and bag of bedding and taken to their assigned housing pod. I had grown tired and wanted out of that nasty cell. After the majority of the men were taken, it was my turn to be processed. I answered the questions to confirm my identity, and was taken into the mysterious room where fifteen men had gone before me. Inside was an open shower, toilet, and sink. I was given soap and instructed to shower, then change into the jail uniform. I was not given any underwear and was told that I would have to keep my own. I saw one pair of large shower shoes on the floor. The female officer told me it was the only pair available. I could not imagine putting my feet into them after all those men. I quickly asked for two sanitary napkins and put them on top of the shower shoes so my bare feet would not touch the floor or the shoes. The look on the officer's face showed she was impressed by my resourcefulness.

She then asked, *"What are you doing here? You don't belong here."*

I replied to her with a tinge of sadness, *"I trusted the wrong man."*

She smiled and nodded as if she could relate to my statement. I was relieved when she left me to shower alone, as I needed the time to gather my thoughts. When she returned, it was to spray me with lice spray.

"Lice spray?" I exclaimed. I cooperated and allowed her to complete the task. After putting on the recycled uniform, I was shown the video, given my bedding and taken to my housing area.

The pod was small compared to Lovejoy. Once again, I was too exhausted to properly evaluate it, and would have to take inventory later. The female officer gave me a private cell because I was a federal inmate. She assigned me to a space in the corner. The predominate feature I noticed was the metal bars that had to be opened so I could enter. The cell was approximately 6x8 feet with a rusted metal bunk and stainless-steel toilet. The desk and stool were bolted to the floor against a concrete wall. I quickly made up my bunk, using the single sheet and very thin blanket I had been given. It was chilly, so I also put on my spare change of clothes to try and keep warm. The mattress was thin and torn at the seams, but I would have to make the best of it.

Just as I was about to get in bed, a young black girl of about twenty came in to introduce herself. She said if I needed anything to let her know. I dismissed her and said I would to speak with her the following day. Several moments later, an announcement was made and each person was told to return to their cells. I was startled by the sound of squeaking bars sliding closed, then slamming locked, but I was grateful to be locked in since I was in a strange place with people I did not know. I had to ball myself into a fetal position to stay warm which was a challenge for me. My desire to sleep was interrupted and delayed by the sound of women singing gospel songs in the cells next to me. Although, they had beautiful voices, I could not enjoy them due to my need for sleep. What seemed like hours passed before they quieted down and I was able to truly rest.

Again, I was awakened by a male officer yelling, "Trays," and the sound of those squeaky bars sliding open. A few moments later, the same young girl from before came to my cell to ask me if I was coming out to eat. When I declined, she asked if she could have my tray, and I told her she could. I was not planning on eating anything while I was in this filthy place. After breakfast, the women returned to their cells at about 6 AM.

Thirty minutes later, an officer returned and yelled, "Supplies!" An inmate retrieved a broom, mop and bucket, along with cleaning solution in spray bottle. I could hear her cleaning the bathroom and shower at the end of the pod. When she finished, she asked me if I wanted to use the supplies to clean my cell. I thanked her and began to sanitize my cell from top to bottom before returning the supplies to the pod for anyone else who wanted to clean.

Since it was still early and most inmates had gone back to bed, I took the opportunity to explore my surroundings. It was obvious to me that the jail itself was very old and neglected. In the center of the pod were three round tables with stools, considered to be the common area for the inmates. It also consisted of two floors with six two-person cells, above and beneath. There was a shower on each floor, but the upstairs one was broken. There was a television, plus two phones on the wall. In a corner were several pairs of shower shoes and clothing left by previous inmates, along with a box filled with a variety of books and bibles.

I learned some of the inmates had been moved in the middle of the night and only eight of us remained. I met a lady who told me how things operated at the jail. All announcements came over the loud speaker and the officers monitored us by camera. She said I could help myself to any of the clothing, shower shoes, and books in the corner. I found a t-shirt and a pair of shower shoes. The previous night, I was given a small hygiene bag with soap, toothpaste, toothbrush, and generic deodorant. After my shower, I washed the t-shirt and shower shoes, then hung them on the top bunk in my cell to dry.

I gathered a bible and a few books from the box and returned to my cell. One by one, the ladies came to introduce themselves to me, all asking the same question.

"What is it like in federal prison?"

"Different," was all I could say.

Funny how they seemed to place me at some type of higher standard because I was a federal inmate. I really just wanted to be left alone, but I soon accepted that being there was part of a larger assignment God had for me that included many tests.

The young black woman I met the previous night returned at lunch time. I declined to eat and she asked for my meal again. When she returned after lunch, I expressed my need for hair products. My hair was still hanging down and was starting to frizz. She returned with her items and I was able to somehow tame my hair. I styled it into two braids with a center part. When

I returned the items, she asked if I would braid hers. I was happy to do it since she had allowed me to use her supplies.

She showed me how to use the phone and order commissary. I contacted my family to add funds to my account so I could order my own supplies. Unfortunately, I had to wait three days to receive them. Once again, my cosmetology skills earned me favor with everyone and I braided hair in exchange for commissary items. On my first day, I got enough food items to last me for the next few days until I received my own.

Braiding hair also provided an opportunity to get to know the ladies. I learned their stories and God allowed me to minister to and pray with them. Each day, someone came to my cell seeking encouragement and a listening ear. It helped to pass the time and after a while the conditions did not seem as bad. My first weekend at the jail, three new women arrived who had been arrested. They had to wait to attend a court hearing the following Monday in order to be released.

Visitation was also on Monday, and my parents, sister, and best friend came. It felt good to be one step closer to home, and they only had to travel an hour to see me. Visitation lasted thirty minutes, and I had to speak to my family through a glass window by telephone. An entirely different experience than what I had been accustomed to in prison. In Aliceville, I could visit with my family for eight hours in an open area. Yes, this place was very different… this was a jail.

The following Monday, my Pastor and good friend from church came to visit. Although he tried hard to hide it, I could see the pain in my Pastor's eyes when he saw me in my jail uniform. My friend was overwhelmed with emotion and did nothing but cry the entire time. My Pastor shared encouraging words and prayed with me before leaving. The visit didn't last long and I tried my best to hold it together the rest of the day. It was difficult to be so close to my loved ones and be left behind to stay in jail. Several weeks passed and I still didn't know my court date.

I was removed from my cell at 4am and taken to the same nasty holding cell I'd occupied when I'd arrived weeks earlier. After waiting several hours, I was handcuffed and put on a van with five men and transported to federal court. After my hearing, I was placed in a large stainless-steel holding area for the rest of the day. It was clean and had a small toilet in the corner and a bench along the wall. I noticed cameras in the ceiling.

I was separated from the men and kept alone for hours, and of course, given that dreadful bag lunch. I could not return to jail until each person completed their hearing. Near the end of the day, a woman my age was put into the cell with me. Her lawyer and the prosecutor had agreed on her house arrest, but the judge had over-ruled them and ordered her to prison for four months. She was completely unprepared to be detained. We shared a few stories and ended up riding back to the jail together. She was really cool and I enjoyed her conversation. Once at the jail, we continued to discuss our faith.

Until my departure, I continued to do hair. The conditions were awful and the food was worse. Mice roamed around at night and I was terrified of them coming into my cell. I sprayed the perimeter of my space with bleach to keep them out. I still had to sleep with a lot of clothes on to keep warm, but by now I had purchased several pairs of thermal underwear and new t-shirts, panties and socks. I had even convinced an officer to give me an extra blanket, but it was confiscated during a shakedown. A shakedown is when your cell is inspected and contraband is removed. Your things are tossed around the cell just like on TV. I was so ready to get out of there.

My lawyer informed me I would have to return to Aliceville to be processed for release from prison. I was not given a timeframe to go by, but I was ready to go back. Being in Aliceville was vacation compared to this journey.

Another week passed and I was awakened at 4am. I distributed my leftover items to the ladies I was leaving behind. It was always bittersweet, because genuine relationships were formed on this journey and my life was impacted by each path I crossed. The loudest and most annoying of all the girls was also told to pack up. Sometimes, she frustrated the other girls, but she had not bothered me. In fact, one day she asked me for prayer.

Today, she was visibly shaken by having to take this journey. I assured her she would be fine and coached her on what to say and what not to say to others. I told her how we would be taunted by the men and would probably have to travel with them. She enjoyed the attention and continued to engage with them which annoyed me, since we were the only two women traveling. I could see the fear in her eyes when we arrived back in Philly to board the plane. Again, nothing can prepare you to be monitored at gunpoint with your hands and feet cuffed. She stayed close to me as if I could somehow protect her. I was confident that God was with me and experienced no fear or anxiety this time around. I was better prepared for the journey than I had been before. I knew the plane would be cold, so I made sure to be layered with two thermal tops and a t-shirt. Just like before, the men boarded first and we were last. There were only six women this time.

The flight seemed longer than the last one and I learned we were heading to Florida to drop off inmates. After that was Oklahoma. I had heard the prison in Oklahoma was very clean, and somewhat of a hub. It had its own private runway and de-boarded inside of the prison. Oklahoma operated like other federal prisons, with similar privileges such as email access, and I could use money already in my BOP account for phone calls and commissary. On the contrary, in jail, I had to have a family member deposit money to my account at each location.

My name was finally called and I looked forward to being in a clean environment again. I exited the rear of the plane and was immediately alarmed when I was directed onto a bus parked outside. The officer told me I was headed to the Grady County Jail. I had heard about the jail in Oklahoma, and everything I had heard was bad. The girl who travelled with me from Virginia was also put on the bus.

When we arrived at the jail, to me, it was far worse than Northern Neck. By now, I was at my breaking point. The other women in the cell appeared to be strung out and high on drugs, as they were laying on the floor. There were flies buzzing about, and puddles of blood. It was a bad, bad scene. For a moment, I think I had a moment of insanity. I asked to speak to a Federal Marshal and reminded him that I was a Federal inmate. I could feel myself tremble and silently prayed that I would not be forced into the cell. The officer said that after the booking process, I would be transferred to the federal housing unit. He allowed me to remain outside of the cell until he was ready to transport me to another building. God had granted me favor, otherwise I would have been put in that cell with the others. When I arrived to the unit, I was stripped searched and given an orange uniform to change into, along with a mattress and bedding.

The housing area was an open space, and I was directed to a bed. Several women came to ask me where I was going. There were others also bound for Aliceville, who were curious about the facility. I talked to them for a few minutes before doing a quick assessment of my surroundings. The restroom was wide open, with no stalls, so no privacy. There were four toilets side by side and a camera was positioned above them. The shower was open with five shower heads attached to the wall. There was no shower curtain or doors. I changed my mind about using the restroom, deciding I would wait until everyone went to bed and the lights were off. I found the phones and made another collect call to my family. I wanted to cry. This was by far the worst place I had been to date, and I had no idea how long I would have to stay.

I began to talk to God, pleading with Him to release me from this situation. I told Him I could not do this, and that I felt like I was going to lose my mind in this place. Like a warm breeze blowing on a summer day, I felt the same sense of peace that I had experienced on previous occasions. I drifted off to sleep and was awakened about three hours later and told to pack my things.

I was searched again and given my travel clothes back to change into, then was loaded on the bus and taken back to the airport. One of the Marshals was surprised to see me, and told me that it was rare for someone to do a 'turn around' meaning to get right back on the plane after a few hours. He said that 'someone above was looking out for me.' I nodded and smiled before getting back on the plane. I could barely contain my gratitude to God for delivering me from the Grady County Jail.

My next stop was back to Lovejoy, Georgia. Off the plane, back on a bus, off the bus, processed, strip searched, and assigned back to the same pod as before. I had a new cellmate this time, but my old one was still there. She found me and thanked me again for the items I had left her. She returned the unopened hygiene products for me to use. I was so happy to get a good hot shower and put on my brand-new soft t-shirt night gown that smelled like fabric softener. I was in a 4-star prison, if there was such a thing. I remained at Lovejoy for another week before I was transported back to Aliceville by bus.

In mid-October 2015, almost one year after surrendering, I was processed and stripped for the last leg of this journey. I returned to the camp with a new girl. I had been traveling for six weeks and had to get all new uniforms, bedding, and a bed assignment, just as if I were new there. Thankfully, I could return to my job in the salon. I had lost so much weight on my road trip that even the size small pants were baggy on me. I was glad to be back to my familiar surroundings among people I was comfortable with. I was also fortunate to have many of my belongings that I had given away returned to me. My items in storage were also returned. I shared little about my journey, and most people respected me enough not to ask.

I asked for a bed assignment in the front of the unit near the door. I didn't know how much longer I would be back in Aliceville, but things got back to normal rather quickly. I rested a few days before returning to work at the salon. Meanwhile, the other ladies at the prison were in the process of putting together a program for breast cancer month. While I was away, they had been preparing for a step show battle between the two units. I wanted to participate and started attending the rehearsals. It was a wonderful experience seeing the women come together for such a great cause. The energy was positive and everyone was busy designing costumes in preparation for the event. There were stories from breast cancer survivors, and many of the women bonded through their experiences. In the end, our unit came out on top, but everyone was a winner that day.

By November, the energy within the prison began to shift due to the upcoming holiday season. Many inmates became sad and depressed this time of year. I admit, I was starting to be discouraged about my release, so I was a bit down as well. I had not heard anything from my attorney and wasn't sure when I would get out. I didn't want to spend another Thanksgiving and Christmas in prison. I hated that they only gave us a bag lunch for dinner, while the officers left to spend the holiday with their families. I tried my best to pass the time by spending more time in the salon, and started taking fitness classes.

On the Tuesday before Thanksgiving, I was paged over the loud speaker to come to the unit counselor's office. When I arrived, she was excited to tell me that she had received my 'order of early release' paperwork. I was caught off guard, because this particular counselor was normally rude to everyone. Surprisingly, she expressed genuine happiness for me. I was told I would be released on the Friday after Thanksgiving. I was overjoyed and tried to contain my excitement without alerting the other women who could see us inside her office. I told the counselor that although I was ecstatic to hear the news, I wanted to be sensitive to the others who had to remain during the holiday season. I asked her to please use discretion regarding my release. I left her office and had to report to the camp secretary to get my travel arrangements. Due to the holiday week, they were anxious to get me processed, because the staff would be out the rest of the week.

Thanksgiving night, I went around to say my goodbyes to the women in both units who I had befriended. I exchanged contact information with many of them, and promised to keep in touch once I got settled. Friday morning at 6am, I reported to the main prison to be processed out of Aliceville Prison. I cried and worshipped God during the entire walk to the other side. I can't articulate my sincere gratitude to God for keeping His promise to me. I was relieved and felt like I had fulfilled each assignment I was given in prison prior to my release. The same way I walked into prison, I left and did not look back. I took away life lessons and gained a personal testimony that has changed my life forever.

Chapter 13

OVERCOMING SPIRITUAL IMPRISONMENT

IMPRISONMENT IS DEFINED AS BEING confined to a state, situation, or place, and having no ability to get out or escape. Imprisonment does not have to be physical... it can be a state of mind. There are many chains that keep us bound, whether in a physical prison or not. Many reading this book will discover that you were already experiencing some form of spiritual imprisonment prior to physical prison. These spiritual prisons come to distract and delay our destiny.

When you have been called by God to fulfill His purpose, the enemy will attempt to keep you locked up—in your mind and emotions. Traps and snares will be set to keep you in isolation and confinement. In my case, I dealt with the prisons of low self-esteem and low self-worth. Although, I often considered myself to be a strong, confident person, I have since come to realize I did not love myself enough to say no to the abusive behavior that had been a part of my life for so many years. Through self-evaluation, I recalled times in my past where I had been abused emotionally, verbally, or physically by a boyfriend. I discovered this had become a pattern of behavior, and that over time I had become comfortable with it and let others set the standard for how I would be treated. I did not fully understand God's unfailing love and was a people pleaser, allowing people to say things to me that today, I would consider disrespectful. I did not know my worth or my true value… and I am still a work in progress.

My biological father was not in my life to teach me the proper way a man should treat a woman. He was not there to show me what love looked like, and had been unfaithful to my mother. The example my mother set for womanhood was to be focused, educated, work hard, and take care of your family. We did not discuss personal relationships in my home as I was growing up. Much of what I learned was through my own life experiences.

With no real understanding of authentic love, I received what I thought was love and accepted poor treatment in my relationships. Over time, I allowed myself to be used, abused and disrespected to the point that it became normal for me. In the federal case that led me to write this book, I was too busy seeking the approval of my ex-fiancé and did not recognize his subtle manipulation and control. I allowed him to define who I was, and lost myself trying to please him. Had I only known how to love myself first, the poor choices that led me to prison could have been prevented from the first 'hello.'

Here are some forms of imprisonment that have been designed to delay our destiny:

Unforgiveness and bitterness will poison our souls. When we choose not to forgive, our hearts become hardened and we become bitter and vengeful. This hinders our spiritual growth and our prayers go unanswered. Unforgiveness also affects our physical bodies, our emotions, and our mental state. It impairs our judgement and our ability to express love to others. A true sign of forgiveness is being able to think of the one who hurt you the worst and not become angry at the thought of them.

Depression is a prison of the mind. It is made up of thoughts, habits and fears that cause mood swings and emotional struggles. In most cases, we tend to isolate ourselves from others and become overtaken by feelings of sadness, hopelessness, and loss of worth.

Self-doubt, low self-esteem, and low self-worth are prisons of the mind, body, and soul. We doubt ourselves when we compare ourselves to others, and lack confidence in our own abilities. We allow others to control and manipulate us when we don't realize our own worth. Self-love begins with accepting God's love. Here is the bible's definition of love:

> *⁴Love is patient, love is kind. It does not envy, it does not boast, it is not proud. ⁵ It does not dishonor others, it is not self-seeking, it is not easily angered, it keeps no record of wrongs. ⁶ Love does not delight in evil but rejoices with the truth. ⁷ It always protects, always trusts, always hopes, always perseveres.⁸ Love never fails. (1Corinthians 9:4-8 NIV)*

Unhealthy relationships — Toxic relationships of any kind are a cancer that eats away at us spiritually, mentally, and emotionally. To remain in these relationships is self-sabotage and reflects one's own willingness to remain imprisoned.

Addictions are over-exposure to things that are not of God. Drugs, excessive eating, pornography, alcoholism, or gambling are a few, but there are many others.

Unfulfilled purposes — The experience of feeling guilty, disappointed, or lost because we are unable to define God's purpose for our lives, which ends up leading to discouragement.

The fear of what others think. Guilt. Shame. Succumbing to these types of fear causes us to hide our gifts and talents, and ultimately delays our destiny because of our own insecurities.

As believers, we must strive to break free from destructive habits and strongholds knowing that our opponent—the devil— seeks to steal, kill, and destroy our future. When we apply the Word of God to our situation, change our thought patterns and speak against ties that bind us, we allow the power of God to change our lives and circumstances. By doing this, we can re-discover our self-worth and be empowered to live our best life.

In addition, when we reject self-condemnation and renew our minds with the Word of God, we are open to discover purpose and gain confidence in God to fulfill it. As a result of doing these things, we can find the courage to say NO to unhealthy relationships, then reject negative thoughts and allow the Holy Spirit to direct our prayers.

In life, we will be presented with many experiences, some will be good and others bad. Before we decide to deny or even resist these experiences or opportunities, we should explore why God chose us in the first place. As we rely on Him for guidance, he reveals to us the possibilities for transformation, and for a much greater outcome. There is always something to learn, and growing from our experiences, we can find freedom in whatever state of being we find ourselves.

Since my release, I have lived a simple, yet rewarding life, and God has continued to be faithful. I am not the person I was before my incarceration. I value things in life I once took for granted—like time and family. My experiences have helped me to realize how valuable I am to God and how much He loves me. I am now confident in who God created me to be and no longer choose to settle for the approval of others, and neither should you. You too can be in control of your own life and be set free from the 'prisons' that keep you bound.

My prison experience has also changed my outlook on life. I have learned many life lessons and had time to consider my mistakes so I am better equipped to make more positive choices going forward. I can't change what has happened in my past, and instead must focus on what God has in store for my future. One of my new favorite scriptures is this: *It was good for me that I was afflicted; that I might learn thy statutes. Psalm 119:71.* I have no complaints nor regrets.

Just as in Genesis 50:20, *everything that the devil intended for my harm, God has worked out for my good.* My life has been greatly blessed by those who God allowed to cross my path. I am a wiser person because of my experiences, and have learned how to trust God completely, no matter how the situation first appears.

Choose to use your time doing things that add value to your life and move you toward the destination God has chosen for you. Trust the process. While others don't always understand my journey, it doesn't matter. It is not important for anyone to understand but me, and I am okay with taking the journey alone if it means fulfilling God's divine purpose in my life.

Chapter 14

GETTING BACK TO NORMAL

AFTER SPENDING ONLY THIRTEEN MONTHS in federal prison, I did not realize my adjustment period after getting out would be such a challenge. I experienced extreme anxiety and episodes of Post-Traumatic Stress Disorder (PTSD) when I returned home. Some mornings when I awoke, I thought I was dreaming. I did not believe I was really at home and was afraid to leave, so I spent most days in my room. I became overwhelmed by my abundance of material things, and realized just how much of it I could live without. Prison taught me how to survive on less and to appreciate everything I have. I no longer take the small things for granted.

In less than a month of my release, I had to have emergency abdominal surgery. Had I still been in prison, I doubt I would have survived. To get medical treatment there is not an urgent matter. I would have had to have been unconscious to be taken seriously, and it may well have been too late. I have seen what happens to people who get sick in prison. It was the grace and timing of God that I was free and able to get the medical care I needed.

Unfortunately, there was not a whole lot of time for me to rest or recover once I got home. I was required to report to my probation officer 72 hours after my release. He also instructed me to get a job within 2 weeks. I was fortunate and blessed to be able to have the support of my parents and church family. Life is much different now. As a convicted felon, I no longer have the privileges I once had like voting rights and applying for a job without having to 'check the box' or disclose criminal history. I am also required to pay restitution, and check in with my probation officer each month. I even must request permission to leave my district, not just the state. As much as I would love to go encourage inmates in the local jails, I am not approved while on probation. Hopefully, that will change soon. With all the things that have come against me, I work that much harder to involve myself in things that I am passionate about. I encourage you to do the same.

Since my release, I have become a community activist and have coordinated various programs for teen girls in my city. To this day, I continue to remain in contact with women I left behind in Aliceville providing moral support and encouragement. My passion to assist women who share my experiences has prompted me to create a business plan to form my own non-profit called We A.D.A.P.T. In addition, I am enrolled in college and completing the degree that I started before my incarceration.

There are many opportunities to ensure a successful re-entry into society, however, they are not always easy to find. The justice system continues to fail us and makes it difficult to be productive citizens after incarceration. The options for employment are limited and shelter is scarce for the returning citizen. It is best to connect with someone with experience who can provide resources and information. There are many programs available to reduce recidivism but most are designed for males.

My mission is to advocate for women returning from incarceration so our voices will be heard and we can get the help needed to have a successful outcome. Will you stand with me? We must stand together and partner with others who share our concerns and visions.

In closing, I encourage you to allow God to use your life—including your hurts and your failures—to fulfill your destiny. Remember, don't allow fear and shame to hold you hostage to your past. Let God get the glory from your story and find purpose in your pain.

May God bless you.

About the Author

With a background that includes over 25 years in the cosmetology field, Trudi has worked in several entrepreneurial situations—from owning a hair salon to an urban art company. In addition, she has served as an Administrator in ministry, working alongside clergy with the goal of expanding community outreach.

Trudi is a contributing author of *Camouflage, Volume 2*, an anthology series. She will soon be releasing her second book entitled, *First Time Offender*. Currently, she has turned her focus to serving others in the areas of advocacy, education and social justice programs. Her passion for the support of inmates and their families led her to form We ADAPT, (We Assist During & After Prison Transition) which provides counsel and resources to individuals before, during, and after incarceration.

Trudi Batiste is a sought-after speaker and the coordinator of "Girl Talk 2.0," a program designed to inspire and motivate underserved youth within her community. She is the mother of three boys and currently resides in Richmond, Virginia.

Contact Information:

www.trudibatiste.com;
www.facebook.com/trudibatiste;
Instagram: @authortrudib
Email: contact@trudibatiste.com

United States Sentencing Guideline Table

Using this table:

The point at which the final offense level and criminal history intersect on the sentencing table determines the defendant's sentencing range.

SENTENCING TABLE
(in months of imprisonment)

	Offense Level	Criminal History Category (Criminal History Points)					
		I (0 or 1)	II (2 or 3)	III (4, 5, 6)	IV (7, 8, 9)	V (10, 11, 12)	VI (13 or more)
Zone A	1	0-6	0-6	0-6	0-6	0-6	0-6
	2	0-6	0-6	0-6	0-6	0-6	1-7
	3	0-6	0-6	0-6	0-6	2-8	3-9
	4	0-6	0-6	0-6	2-8	4-10	6-12
	5	0-6	0-6	1-7	4-10	6-12	9-15
	6	0-6	1-7	2-8	6-12	9-15	12-18
Zone B	7	0-6	2-8	4-10	8-14	12-18	15-21
	8	0-6	4-10	6-12	10-16	15-21	18-24
	9	4-10	6-12	8-14	12-18	18-24	21-27
	10	6-12	8-14	10-16	15-21	21-27	24-30
	11	8-14	10-16	12-18	18-24	24-30	27-33
Zone C	12	10-16	12-18	15-21	21-27	27-33	30-37
	13	12-18	15-21	18-24	24-30	30-37	33-41
	14	15-21	18-24	21-27	27-33	33-41	37-46
	15	18-24	21-27	24-30	30-37	37-46	41-51
	16	21-27	24-30	27-33	33-41	41-51	46-57
	17	24-30	27-33	30-37	37-46	46-57	51-63
	18	27-33	30-37	33-41	41-51	51-63	57-71
	19	30-37	33-41	37-46	46-57	57-71	63-78
	20	33-41	37-46	41-51	51-63	63-78	70-87
	21	37-46	41-51	46-57	57-71	70-87	77-96
	22	41-51	46-57	51-63	63-78	77-96	84-105
	23	46-57	51-63	57-71	70-87	84-105	92-115
	24	51-63	57-71	63-78	77-96	92-115	100-125
	25	57-71	63-78	70-87	84-105	100-125	110-137
	26	63-78	70-87	78-97	92-115	110-137	120-150
Zone D	27	70-87	78-97	87-108	100-125	120-150	130-162
	28	78-97	87-108	97-121	110-137	130-162	140-175
	29	87-108	97-121	108-135	121-151	140-175	151-188
	30	97-121	108-135	121-151	135-168	151-188	168-210
	31	108-135	121-151	135-168	151-188	168-210	188-235
	32	121-151	135-168	151-188	168-210	188-235	210-262
	33	135-168	151-188	168-210	188-235	210-262	235-293
	34	151-188	168-210	188-235	210-262	235-293	262-327
	35	168-210	188-235	210-262	235-293	262-327	292-365
	36	188-235	210-262	235-293	262-327	292-365	324-405
	37	210-262	235-293	262-327	292-365	324-405	360-life
	38	235-293	262-327	292-365	324-405	360-life	360-life
	39	262-327	292-365	324-405	360-life	360-life	360-life
	40	292-365	324-405	360-life	360-life	360-life	360-life
	41	324-405	360-life	360-life	360-life	360-life	360-life
	42	360-life	360-life	360-life	360-life	360-life	360-life
	43	life	life	life	life	life	life

November 1, 2012

FAMM (Families Against Mandatory Minimums) is a nonprofit, nonpartisan organization fighting for smart sentencing laws that protect public safety. www.famm.org

Families Against Mandatory Minimums
1100 H Street NW
Suite 1000
Washington, D.C. 20005

If you have loved ones who are incarcerated in federal prison who wish to receive updates from FAMM, please tell them to add famm@famm.org to their email account.

Prison Legal News is a 72-page magazine that reports on criminal justice issues and prison and jail-related civil litigation, with an emphasis on prisoners' rights. To subscribe: www.prisonlegalnews.org

Prison Legal News
P.O. Box 1151
1013 Lucerne Ave
Lake Worth, FL 33460
Phone: 561-360-2523
info@prisonlegalnews.org

Prison Talk is an information and inmate family support group. www.prisontalk.com

---

Easily send free photos to inmates from your phone. www.pigeon.ly

---

Magazine subscription service for inmates for a full year: www.inmatemagazineservice.com

Bible Study Correspondence Courses
You must write to request these studies.

Great Hope Bible Institute
Great Hope Ministries
PO Box 472
Wimberley, TX 78676
A series of correspondence courses for children, teens, young adults, adults, or advanced students published by The Mailbox Club. Certificate awarded upon completion of each course.
www.greathope.org

Crossroad Bible Institute
Attention: Correspondence Program
PO Box 900
Grand Rapids, MI 49509-0900
www.crossroadbibleinstitute.org

Tier 1 includes 50 truths of the Christian faith within a 12-lesson format. Certificate and letter of congratulations from the President of Crossroads Bible Institute upon completion. In Tier 2, each student is placed with his or her own personal instructor who will serve as the student's mentor throughout the 3-course study, which includes: Ten Men You Should Know, In God We Trust, and The Sermon on the Mount. Graduation certificate upon completion of each course.

Lamp and Light Publishers, Inc.
26 Road 5577
Farmington, MN 89401-1436

Free Bible Study Correspondence include: The First Step, Stepping Stones to God, Seven Steps to Obedience, In Step with the Prince of Peace, The Faith Worth Dying for, The Heavenly Pilgrimage, Studying His Word, Praying to Him, Committed to

Him, Worshipping Him, Fasting for His Glory, Discerning God's Will, Witnessing for Him, Building Christian Homes, The Life of Christian Stewardship, So, were the Churches established, Managing His Money, Christian Brotherhood, and Shepherding the Sheep.

The Salvation Army
Correctional Services Bureau
PO Box C-635
West Nyack, NY 10994-1739
A set curriculum with six courses offered in the following order: The Gospel of John, The Christian Life, The Early Church (a study of the book of Acts), Early Beginnings (a study of the book of Genesis), The Birth of a Nation (a study of the history of Israel), and a Bible Survey Course. Certificate provided upon completion of each course. A letter of congratulations, a final certificate, a Bible engraved with the student's name, and an invitation to participate in the Advanced Curriculum is given upon completion of all 6 courses. The Advanced Curriculum includes courses in the Advent of Jesus Christ, Footsteps to Calvary, Tabernacle Types and Teachings, The Priesthood-Old and New, A Brief Study of the Psalms, and the Greatest Plan. A certificate is given for completion of each course and a pocket size NKJ Bible when all six courses are finished. These lessons also come in Spanish.

The Voice of Prophecy
PO Box 53055
Los Angeles, CA 90053
www.vop.com
805.955.7611
This basic Bible course is called, "Discover Bible Guides." Discover answers hundreds of questions that effect your life from a source you can trust – the Bible. The newest Bible course is, "Focus on Prophecy", which includes a 20-lesson in-depth study on Daniel and Revelation.

Exodus Prison Ministry
Bible Correspondence Studies
PO Box 6363
Lubbock, TX 79493

Bible College Through Correspondence
A fee is required for the following courses:

Promise Ministries, Inc.
Center for Biblical Studies
PO Box 177
Battle Creek, MI 49016-0177
www.pmiministries.com

Distance Bible and Pastoral Ministry Training
Promise Ministries, Inc. offers the following degrees through their Center for Biblical Studies correspondence courses:

First Year - Counselor of Biblical Studies (30 credit hours)
Second Year - Associate of Biblical Studies (60 credit hours)
Third Year - Graduate of Biblical Studies (90 credit hours)
Fourth Year - Bachelor Of Biblical Studies (120 credit hours)
Fifth Year - Master of Biblical Studies (180 credit hours)
Sixth Year - Doctor of Biblical Studies (210 credit hours)

Tuition at the PMI Center for Biblical Studies is currently $30 per credit hour or $1000 per year. PMI commits to work with you in any way possible in order to help you enroll and study God's Word. This includes, but is not limited to, payment plans as low as $15 per month and partial or full scholarships. Write to them and received a full description of their program, a copy of their curriculum, and an application for enrollment.

Global University
1211 South Glenstone Ave.
Springfield, MO 65804

Global University(Berean) offers over 70 non-degree courses with four different diploma options. Tuition is waived for incarcerated students and they received a 25 percent discount on all materials. The average cost per course is $25. Berean also offers 4 different Associate of Arts and 9 different Bachelor of Arts degrees. The average cost per course with the inmate discount is $200. Three Master of the Arts degrees are available for an average cost of $400 per course.

Moody Bible Institute
Distance Learning Center
820 North La Salle Boulevard
Chicago, IL 60610-3284

The Moody Bible Institute offers a number of Independent Study degree programs at regular costs. Of particular interest to incarcerated believers is the over 60 "Continuing Education Unit" courses that they offer through correspondence for only $49 each plus $12 for all shipping and postage costs. These are college level courses offered on every book of the Old and New Testament and a variety of other subjects.

Correspondence Certificate Program for Inmates

Blackstone Paralegal Studies
P.O. Box 3717
Allentown, PA 18106
www.blackstone.edu
info@blackstone.edu

Undergraduate Correspondence College Program for Inmates:

Adams State University
Andrews University
Louisiana State University

Ohio University
University of N. Carolina
Upper Iowa University

Recommended Scripture Readings
New International Version

Psalm 18:23 *I have been blameless before him and have kept myself from sin.*

Matthew 5:16 *In the same way, let your light shine before others, that they may see your good deeds and glorify your Father in heaven.*

Psalm 13:6 *I will sing the LORD's praise, for he has been good to me.*

James 4:7-8 *Submit yourselves, then, to God. Resist the devil, and he will flee from you. Come near to God and He will come near to you.*

Psalm 23:1 *The LORD is my shepherd, I lack nothing.*

1 Thessalonians 5:16-18 *Rejoice always, pray continually, give thanks in all circumstances; for this is God's will for you in Christ Jesus.*

Psalm 145:17 *The LORD is righteous in all his ways and faithful in all He does.*

Jeremiah 29:13-14 *You will seek me and find me when you seek me with all your heart. I will be found by you," declares the LORD, "and will bring you back from captivity"*

1 Corinthians 2:9 *What no eye has seen, what no ear has heard, and what no human mind has conceived the things God has prepared for those who love him.*

Psalm 18:2-3 *The LORD is my rock, my fortress and my deliverer; my God is my rock, in whom I take refuge, my shield and the horn of my salvation, my stronghold. I called to the LORD, who is worthy of praise, and I have been saved from my enemies.*

1 Samuel 16:7 *The LORD does not look at the things people look at. People look at the outward appearance, but the LORD looks at the heart."*

Psalm 46:1 *God is our refuge and strength, an ever-present help in trouble.*

Ephesians 2:8-9 *For it is by grace you have been saved, through faith—and this is not from yourselves, it is the gift of God— not by works, so that no one can boast.*

Romans 8:1 *Therefore, there is now no condemnation for those who are in Christ Jesus*

Psalm 32:7 *You are my hiding place; you will protect me from trouble and surround me with songs of deliverance.*

Hebrews 13:5 *Never will I leave you; never will I forsake you.*

Psalm 68:19-20 *Praise be to the Lord, to God our Savior, who daily bears our burdens. Our God is a God who saves; from the Sovereign LORD comes escape from death.*

Matthew 5:16 *In the same way, let your light shine before others, that they may see your good deeds and glorify your Father in heaven.*

2 Corinthians 4:18 *So we fix our eyes not on what is seen, but on what is unseen, since what is seen is temporary, but what is unseen is eternal.*

Psalm 145:13 *Your kingdom is an everlasting kingdom, and your dominion endures through all generations. The LORD is trustworthy in all He promises and faithful in all He does.*

Glossary

Admissions and Orientation (A&O) – Inmates are given rules and expectations for prison.

Arraignment hearing – A court hearing where one is informed of charges and may plead guilty or not guilty.

Arrest – To take a person into custody with the purpose of charging them with a criminal offense.

Assistant United States Attorney (AUSA) – A top federal law enforcement official also known as a prosecuting attorney in federal criminal cases.

Bail – An amount determined by the court to guarantee appearance at future court hearings.

Base offense level- the starting point for determining the seriousness of an offense.

Bond – An alternative for jail for those charged with a federal crime.

Community service – Unpaid work required instead of going to prison.

Commissary – A store that sells basic food and supplies in prison.

Complaint – a statement written by a federal prosecutor accusing you of a crime.

Conspiracy – a secret plan between two or more to carry out an illegal act.

Contraband – An illegal substance or object.

Conviction – A judgement of guilt against a criminal defendant.

Counsel – A legal advisor or another name for attorney.

Count – An allegation in an indictment. Each allegation is referred to as a count.

Court assessment fee – A fee for any person convicted of an offense by the United States.

Criminal record/history – A list of crimes one has previously committed.

Defendant – An individual whom a pending criminal proceeding is against.

Designation package – A letter that addresses the location of the facility one must surrender to.

Detainment – To be held in a local jail to await trial date.

Discovery – Methods used to gather information and facts as evidence in preparation for trial.

Downward motion – A form of a lesser sentence that a judge may consider.

Evidence – The means by with an allegation may be proven such as oral testimony, documents, or objects.

Federal Bureau of Prisons (FBOP) – An institution that manages federal prisons.

Federal court – A court established by the authority of the federal government.

Federal National Lockbox – A type of bank account that receives and distributes funds to inmates.

Federal prison camp – A minimum security institution for inmates who do not pose threat for violence or escape.

Federal Sentencing Guideline Chart – A table that is used to tell judges the appropriate sentencing range for most crimes

Felony – A crime serious enough to be punishable by death or a period in federal or state prison.

Furlough - Temporary release from prison.

Good time conduct (GTC) – Time deducted for good time which is equal to forty-seven days or 15% of sentence.

Grand Jury – A panel of citizens in who convene to decide if the government should proceed with prosecution of someone who is suspected of a crime.

Halfway House – A residential facility for those who have been released from incarceration to help adjust to re-entering the community.

Home Confinement – To be restricted to home, often with electronic monitoring, and only authorized to leave with approval.

Indictment – A formal written statement issued by a grand jury and signed by a federal prosecutor accusing one or more of a crime.

Inmate - A term used to describe one in custody of jail or prison.

Jail – A facility that has been designed to hold individuals who are awaiting trial or who are serving sentences less than one year.

Jurors – A group of persons who have been selected to hear evidence and render a verdict on a criminal matter and recommend a sentence.

Magistrate judge - A federal judge who assist district judges with their duties. Usually the first judge the defendant appears before.

Mandatory release – An inmate has served the legally required portion of the sentence.

Mandatory sentence – A specified number of years imposed for specific crimes.

Motions - A written or oral application made to a *court* or judge to obtain a ruling or order directing that some act be done in favor of the applicant.

Pardon - An act of clemency that absolves one from legal consequences of crime and/or conviction.

Plea - A formal response by the defendant to the charges of the prosecutor in a criminal case.

Plea bargain - A defendant will plead guilty to the original or other charge in return for some concession from the prosecutor.

Pre-sentencing Investigation (PSI)/ Pre-sentencing Report (PSR) – A written report used to assist the court in determining and appropriate sentence and post-incarceration instructions.

Pretrial phase – The three phases include: to collect and analyze defendant information, to make recommendations to the court concerning conditions of release, and to supervise defendants who are released from secure custody.

Pre-trial bond officer – An officer who monitor the activities and behavior in the pre-trial phase.

Prison – A secure facility operated by state or federal government where adult felons are incarcerated.

Probable cause – A belief based on facts that a crime has been committed

Probation – To remain in the community under supervision after being convicted of a crime.

Prosecutor - One who prosecutes for a crime in the name of the government.

PTSD – A psychological condition resulting from traumatic events that evokes fear, terror, and helplessness.

Register ID number – The eight-digit number assigned to inmates by the federal bureau of prisons.

Recidivism – To be arrested for a new offense and returned to prison.

Recommendation – Suggestions to the court regarding one's conditions of release.

Release on Recognizance (ROR) – A release from custody based on the defendant's written promise to appear.

Remanded – To be arrested.

Residential Drug Abuse Program (RDAP) - A voluntary, 500-hour, 9 to12-month program for federal prisoners with substance abuse problems. Completion of program may result in sentence reduction.

Restitution – The act of compensating for loss, damages, or injury.

Security level – The state of federal inmates can be designated as low, medium, high, or special.

Sentence – A sanction ordered by the court.

Special Housing Unit (SHU) – To be in isolation in prison.

Subpoena – A written order requiring one to appear in court.

Suspect – one who is suspected of having committed a crime

Target Letter – An official notice from the government that you are suspected of a serious crime.

Testify – To state or affirm testimony in a legal case.

Trial- A proceeding which the government and defense present evidence to prove or disprove charges in a case

U. S. Marshal – An armed officer who transports federal inmates.

Variance – A discrepancy in two documents between the charge and the evidence presented.

Victim impact statement – Victims will voice their trauma and victimization resulting from criminal actions of the offender.

Witness:One who can give a firsthand account of something seen, heard, or experienced

Notes

The vision of **We A.D.A.P.T.** is to bring help, hope, emotional, and spiritual support to individuals and their families prior to, during, and after prison transition.

The mission of **We A.D.A.P.T.** is to empower and encourage potential offenders and formerly incarcerated individuals to transform their lives and the communities around them.

Educate | Motivate | Inspire

Invite Trudi to your next event or obtain support for your ministry, family, or loved one who is incarcerated.

Contact @ trudibatiste.com